Mandy G.

GW01606650

Francis King has written numerous books on the borderlands of religion, politics and science; he has also contributed to reference works such as the *Encyclopedia of Mythology* and the *Encyclopedia of the Unexplained.* He considers the current wave of irrationalism, in which the occult revival is of some importance, to be symptomatic of certain destructive tendencies in western society, the full importance of which has still to be appreciated by psychologists, sociologists and theologians.

Now a freelance writer, Isabel Sutherland has spent many years in journalism and book publishing. She became interested in the occult as a detached observer when working as deputy editor of the encyclopedia of the supernatural, *Man, Myth and Magic.*

The Rebirth of Magic

Francis King and Isabel Sutherland

CORGI BOOKS
A DIVISION OF TRANSWORLD PUBLISHERS LTD

THE REBIRTH OF MAGIC

A CORGI BOOK 0 552 11880 X

First publication in Great Britain

PRINTING HISTORY
Corgi edition published 1982

Copyright © Francis King and Isabel Sutherland 1982

This book is set in 10/11 English Times

Corgi Books are published by
Transworld Publishers Ltd.,
Century House, 61–63 Uxbridge Road,
Ealing, London, W5 5SA

Printed in Great Britain by
Hunt Barnard Printing, Aylesbury, Bucks.

Contents

1 *Introducing the Magicians*

Some three years or so ago *Prediction*, a popular occult monthly, published a query from one of its readers. He and his wife were, he wrote, 'crazy about rituals and ritual magic' and ceremonially consecrated all their most treasured possessions. They had recently installed a telephone in their home and were anxious to bless it with the appropriate rite. What god, demon, or other non-human entity, asked the enquirer, should be invoked into his telephone?

The editor of the magazine's problem page was in no way flustered or surprised by this question. Telephones, the correspondent was informed, were a means of communication and were therefore attributed to the Graeco-Egyptian god Thoth-Hermes. It was this god, or Mercury, his Roman equivalent, who should be induced to bless and consecrate the telephone. If, however, added the *Prediction* journalist, his reader was inclined to 'qabalistic magic' he should approach the matter through 'Hod', the eighth 'sephirah' of *Otz Chiim*, the qabalistic symbol identified with the Tree of Life, using the appropriate incenses, symbols and Divine Names.

The magician who wanted to submit his telephone to occult influences attracted the attention of Michael Wharton, expert on such seemingly diverse matters as the economic theories of Major Douglas, Ossian's poetry, ayurvedic dentistry, and the more endearingly daft aspects of the current occult boom. It was hopeless, asserted Mr. Wharton, for this dedicated ritualist to expect any visible appearance of Thoth-Hermes, Mercury, or even Hod, as a result of his ceremonial endeavours. If any objective phenomenon did take place it would only be a physical manifestation of Buzby – the loathsome fowl inexplicably used by the public relations industry in order to advertise the overpriced and overmanned British telephone system.

Ludicrous as Mr. Wharton, perhaps rightly, considered question and answer, both are not without significance and interest. For they illustrate the extent of the current magical revival and its influence on those inclined to occult studies. *Prediction* has been published since before World War II, but until about twenty five years or so ago references to ritual magic were rarely found in its pages; today they are to be found in almost every issue.

An even stronger indication of the interest in ritual magic at the present day is provided by the catalogues issued by such mail order suppliers of occult books and impedimenta as 'Sorcerer's Apprentice' (Leeds, England) and 'Magickal Childe' (New York). As well as the usual books and tarot decks there are advertised crescent-bladed knives, for ritually cutting herbs and magic circles, incenses dedicated to various gods, angels and demons, cast-iron cauldrons, damiana ('the psychic aphrodisiac'), candles, symbolically coloured or realistically shaped to resemble phalli of such immensity as to risk inducing feelings of inadequacy in most of their male purchasers, and cassette-tapes of Aleister Crowley ('the Master Therion') reciting an invocation in the 'Angelic Language' produced by the Elizabethan magicians John Dee and Edward Kelly.

The ordinary man or woman is often vaguely aware of the current craze amongst some people, particularly young people, for magic and witchcraft. For, from time to time, the more downmarket British and American newspapers will report the occurrence of sacrilegious acts in deserted churches and burial grounds – these are usually attributed to 'satanists' or 'black witches' – or reproduce blurry photographs of cultists, sometimes exotically robed, sometimes naked and, when female, equipped with breasts and buttocks of notable size and rotundity.

Usually these alleged magicians or witches bear ritual swords, daggers and other mystic implements. They are unconcerned by the presence of a press photographer at the celebration of their inmost mysteries.

The most interesting of the many groups that play such an important part in the modern rebirth of western magic shun press publicity. The practices engaged in by their members may be eccentric by ordinary standards but they are sincerely performed with perfectly serious ends in view – the attainment of power and wisdom, the transmutation of the lead of the everyday personality into the gold of adepthood.

To describe in detail all these groups would be impossible, for, apart from the sheer immensity of the task, it is probable that the very existence of many of them is unknown to any outsider. It is possible, however, to differentiate between three important strands in contemporary associations practising ritual magic. Firstly, the strand of 'orthodox' western magic as transmitted from the past to the present, albeit in distorted and modified form, by the Hermetic Order of the Golden Dawn and its immediate successors. Secondly, the strand of 'Thelemic Magic' – the intellectually impressive although, perhaps, morally dubious, synthesis of old European occultism, new daemonic religion of 'Force and Fire', and tantric (sexual) yoga created by Aleister Crowley. Thirdly, the strand of magic influenced by the writings of the late Dr. Margaret Murray and her admirers amongst those most active in modern witchcraft.

Let us look in each category at a 'composite' group – that is to say a group which, although not actually existing in the precise form described, combines features from all the groups in its category and thus illustrates the common factors of the 'strand'.

The Order of the Secret Rose is a London-based occult group deriving from the tradition of the Golden Dawn, an occult society of the last century whose importance has been aptly summed up by Israel Regardie – himself an initiate of the late offshoot of the Order – in the follow-

Title page of *The Book of the Sacred Magic of Abra-Melin the Mage*, 1898 edition.

ing words: 'There can be little or no doubt that the Golden Dawn is, (or rather was until recently) the sole depository of western magical knowledge, the only Magical Order of any real worth that the West in our time has known. A great many other occult organizations owe what little magical knowledge is theirs to leakages from that Order and its renegade members'.

The story of the Golden Dawn is outlined in later chapters of this book, as are its occult teachings and practices; but it does seem worth emphasizing that so far as the English-speaking world is concerned Regardie's contention is undoubtedly correct. Of the dozens of small magical fraternities existing today many owe their existence, doctrines, and rituals to the initiates of the Golden Dawn. It is true, of course, that some of these organizations claim to have evolved independently and to be 'older than the Golden Dawn', but such claims are not backed up by documentation and, in view of the remarkable resemblance between their teachings and those of the earlier Order, they must be disregarded until the production of hard evidence in their favour.

The Secret Rose has between twenty and thirty members and a permanent home 'somewhere south of the Thames'. Here the Order engages in the traditional pursuits of the western magician, its initiates consecrating talismans – charms designed for a specific purpose rather than for general good luck – invoking Angels, casting spells designed to produce invisibility,[1] evoking spirits to visible appearance, and so on.

Its Supreme Magus is 'Butch' Metzger-Bouchere, an insurance broker whose fellow businessmen are quite unaware of his occult beliefs and activities and regard him as 'sound but dull'. It is unlikely that they would even recognize him if they saw him at one of the festivals of his Secret Rose. On, for example, the day of Corpus Christi, when, clad in a black robe and with an iron chain round his neck, he is lashed to a Calvary Cross from whence to recite an oath on behalf of the entire body of initiates:

> I do this day spiritually bind myself on behalf of the entire membership of the Order.
>
> That I will do the utmost to lead a pure and unselfish life. . . .
>
> That I will keep secret all things connected with the Order and its Occult Wisdom. . . .
>
> That I will uphold to the utmost the authority of the Chiefs of the Order. . . .

Furthermore, that I will perform all practical magical workings connected with this Order in a place concealed and apart from the gaze of the outer and uninitiated world, and that I will not display our magical implements, nor reveal their use, but will keep secret this Inner Rosicrucian Wisdom even as the same has been kept secret through the ages; that I will not make any symbol or Talisman in the Flashing Colours for any uninitiated person without a special permission from the Chiefs of the Order. That I will only perform any practical magic before the uninitiated which is of a simple and already well-known nature; and that I will show them no secret mode of working, keeping strictly concealed from them our methods of Tarot and other divination, of clairvoyance, of astral projection, of the consecration of talismans and symbols, of the Rituals of the Pentagram and the Hexagram, and, most especially, of the use and attribution of the Flashing Colours and the vibratory mode of pronouncing the Divine Names.

I promise and swear that I will apply myself to the Great Work, the purification and exaltation of my spiritual nature so that with the Divine Aid I may at length attain to be more than human. . . .

I furthermore solemnly pledge myself never to work at any important symbol without first invoking the highest Divine Names connected therewith, and especially not to debase my knowledge of practical magic to purposes of evil and selfseeking. If I break this oath I invoke the avenging Angel HVA that the evil may react on me.

I furthermore promise that I will always display brotherly love and forbearance towards the members of the Whole Order. . . .

I also undertake to work unassisted at the subjects prescribed for study. . . .

Finally, if I should meet one who claims to be a member of this Order I will examine him with care before acknowledging him or her to be such.

I invoke Thee, Thou great avenging Angel HVA to confirm and strengthen all the members of this Order during the ensuing revolution of the Sun; to keep them steadfast in the path of rectitude and self sacrifice and to confer upon them the power of discernment, that they may choose between good and evil and try all things with sure knowledge and judgment.

This sonorous and long-winded oath gives a good idea of the sort of magical operations undertaken by the initiates of Orders such as the Secret Rose. By 'the Flashing Colours' is meant the use of a basic colour and its complementary colour (for example red and green, or orange and blue) as a means of hypnosis. By the 'consecration of talismans' is meant the performance of a ritual designed to 'charge' a specially prepared symbol with the powers of a spiritual entity in much the same way that a battery is charged with electricity. The 'Rituals of the Pentagram and the Hexagram' are ceremonies at which simple geometrical figures are traced in the air at the same time as various Hebrew Divine Names (for example Adonai, 'Lord', or Ahih, 'I am') are spoken in a particularly solemn chant known as 'Vibration'. These rites are supposed to have the power of attracting (invoking) or repelling (banishing) various types of spiritual force as symbolized by the signs of the zodiac, the planets etc. The supposed name and nature of the 'great avenging Angel HVA' whose invocation is the climax of the oath requires some explanation. In the Hebrew qabalah HVA (spelt He, Vau, Aleph in Hebrew) is a mystical name applied to Kether, the 'Crown' of the mystic glyph known as the Tree of Life and considered to symbolize the highest aspect of manifested Deity. Thus on one level the invocation of HVA is simply swearing by God. In Hebrew, however, the twenty-two letters of the alphabet have a numerical as well as a consonantal significance and the letters of the name HVA represent, from left to right, the numbers five, six and one. It is on this basis that the members of the western magical orders give a secondary interpretation to the name HVA. Five, they say is the number of man himself as the microcosm or 'little world'. Six is the number of the macrocosm, the 'great world', meaning not just the physical universe but all the manifested aspects of God. One is the number of unity and perfection. The name HVA therefore represents, so it is claimed, the ultimate goal of the magician – the union between subject and object, microcosm and macrocosm, God and man.

The social composition of orders such as the Secret Rose is far from homogeneous. Their initiates include not only conventional 'professional' men and women, but such people as electricians, housewives, and taxi-drivers. At first sight this seems an incongruous mish-mash of individuals having little in common with one another. Nevertheless, fellow initiates tend to display towards one another an affection and a solidarity that cuts right across class-barriers. They attend one another's weddings, christenings and other family occasions, they call each other by their first names, and they give each other Christmas and even birthday presents. To use their own occult terminology, they have built up their Order into a 'Group-soul', a living organism in which the whole is greater than the sum of its constituent parts. They are united by their fervent belief that, as one of them has said, in ritual magic they have found 'not only a key to the enigmas of the universe but a method which enables them to transcend the limits of ordinary consciousness, to transmute the dry victuals of everyday existence into the Bread of Life and ultimately to attain unto that Divine Union which is the goal of mystic and magician alike'.

We will call our second composite group – the one which illustrates the strand of 'thelemic magic', the Order of Oz. 'Oz' is, of course, a word which has slightly risible undertones for many people, who inevitably associate it with Kansas 'twisters', tin men, the late Judy Garland and yellow brick roads. Nevertheless, the word is important to all thelemic magicians, for it is not derived from childrens' stories, but from the numerical qabalah. In Hebrew the word Oz is spelt with the Hebrew letters Ayin and Zayin and by gematria – the qabalists' technique of turning letters into numbers – adds up to seventy seven.

According to Aleister Crowley, the greatest of all occult teachers as far as thelemic magicians are concerned, this number represents magic acting on the world of matter. This is because it can be expressed as eleven, the grand number of ritual magic, multiplied by seven, the number of manifestation. In addition to this the word Oz has sexual – indeed satanic – undertones. For its first letter (Ayin) represents the male goat, that zestful symbol of rampant and joyful lust worshipped at the legendary Witches' Sabbath and identified by Crowley with Trump XV of the tarot deck, the ithyphallic 'Devil' which, for many western magicians, is a symbol of dense matter and its limitations.

The short manifesto known as *Liber Oz* is the basic creed of many of the thelemic magical orders of the type represented by our composite group. This reads as follows:

LIBER OZ

There is no God but man! Deus homo est!

1. Man has the right to live by his own law:
   to live in the way that he wills to do:
   to work as he will:
   to play as he will:
   to rest as he will:
   to die when and how he will.
2. Man has the right to eat what he will:
   to drink what he will:
   to dwell where he will:
   to move as he will on the face of the earth.
3. Man has the right to think what he will:
   to speak what he will:
   to draw, paint, carve, etc. mould, build as he will:
   to dress as he will.
4. Man has the right to love as he will:
   "take your fill and will of love as ye will,
   when, where and with whom ye will". AL.I.51

5. Man has the right to kill those who would thwart these rights.
   "the slaves shall serve". AL.I.57

The quotations which end sections four and five of *Oz* are from *Liber AL*, the *Book of the Law*, the supreme holy book of the new religion of Thelema devised by Crowley himself.

Crowley is best remembered by the general public as 'the wickedest man in the world' (a title conferred upon him in the twenties by the Hearst and Beaverbrook press) as an individual who had actually lived out the sexual fantasies that most people keep to themselves. In reality he was the creator of a highly intellectual and complex system of occultism, having some similarities with certain aspects of both medieval Eastern European dualism and the subtle philosophy and accepted practice of Bengali tantricism. A brief account of this system is given in later chapters, but it is likely that few save Crowley himself have mastered the system in its entirety.

It is not, therefore, surprising that the men and women who are the rank and file of such Crowleyan societies as our 'composite' Order of Oz largely confine their attentions to those parts of the 'Magick' – for so Crowley's system is often called – which have the most personal appeal. Such people tend to be familiar with even the obscurest writings of their Master, but few of them work at his intensely demanding techniques of psycho-spiritual development in anything but a desultory way. Even the sexo-yogic practices which are such an important part of Magick are sometimes neglected and it is likely that some of the members of Crowleyan groups are more attracted by the glamour of dressing up in exotic vestments and of belonging to a secret society than they are by the prospect of achieving any real magical results – always supposing, of course, that such results are capable of achievement.

The principal group activity of most of the societies typified by our composite Order of Oz are their celebrations of the 'Gnostic Catholic Mass' as revised and translated from German into English by Crowley himself.

The version of the Gnostic Catholic Mass usually performed is at least semi-respectable and lies somewhere between the almost bourgeois conventionality of the present day Swiss-German rite, in which both Priest and Priestess remain fully clothed throughout the ceremony, and the wild impropriety of a Californian Gnostic group which flourished twenty or thirty years ago and made an act of cunnilingus the central point of its recension of the Mass. That is to say, in the ritual as carried out by most contemporary groups the Priest and Priestess are naked for part of the ceremony, but when the rubric demands that 'the Priest shall plunge his Lance into the Chalice borne by the Priestess' – which some believe to imply that the two should copulate together – this injunction is obeyed literally and not symbolically, the Priest merely dipping a short spear into a cup of wine carried by the Priestess.

One of us has twice witnessed such watered-down versions of the Gnostic Mass and, in spite of the rather dismal surroundings in which they were celebrated, they were still quite impressive as pure theatre. Even the scenery was fairly good; at the north end of the room was a scarlet-draped altar, seven feet wide and almost four feet high. On it were a splendidly bound copy of Crowley's *Liber vel Legis*, six candles flaring on either side of it, a huge silver cup of wine, and a plate bearing cakes of a peculiar appearance and consistency. The altar supported a smaller 'super-altar' on which rested a highly coloured, hand-painted reproduction on wood of ancient Egyptian symbols. This was flanked by eight more candles. The Priest was clothed in a white cowled robe, the Priestess in a white robe with a scarlet sash and a blue cowl.

The rites began with the congregation reciting the Gnostic Creed, a heavily 'Crowleyanized' version of a statement of belief used by the French Gnostic Church of almost eighty years ago and admirably summarizing the beliefs of the devotees of Magick:

> I believe in One Secret and Ineffable Lord; in One Star of whose Fire we are created and to which Fire we shall

return; in one Father of Life, Mystery of Mystery, sole viceregent of the Sun upon Earth; and in one Air, nourisher of all that breathes.

And I believe in one Earth, Mother of us all; and in one Womb wherein all men are begotten, and wherein they shall all rest.

And I believe in the Serpent and the Lion; and in the Communion of the Saints.

And I believe one Gnostic and Catholic Church of Life, Light, Liberty and Love, the Word of whose Law is THELEMA (Will).

And I believe in the Miracle of the Mass.

And I confess one Baptism of Wisdom whereby we accomplish the Miracle of Incarnation.

And I confess my life one, individual and eternal.

After a good deal of esoteric flim-flam between the Priest and the Priestess – aptly described by one American observer as 'Grail-stuff' – the eleven Collects were recited. These bore no resemblance to those of Catholic Christianity and included invocations of the Sun, the Earth, and the 'Saints' amongst whom was Ulrich von Hutten, the syphilitic 16th–century Lutheran knight, Alexander VI, the incestuous Borgia Pope, and Ludwig, the mad homosexual King of Bavaria.

Following this the elements – i.e. the wine and the unappetizing cakes to which we have previously referred – were consecrated as 'the Blood and Body of God'. After an anthem, chanted irritatingly off-key, Priest, Priestess and congregation communicated, each drinking a whole cup of wine, and eating a whole cake. The cakes were, in fact, baked from a mixture of flour, honey, red wine and human blood; Crowley claimed that the best blood for this purpose was 'that of the moon, monthly', i.e., menstrual blood, but on the occasions on which one of us was present the blood of the Priest had been used. Nevertheless, the taste of the cakes was repellent.

The ceremony concluded with the Priest giving his 'magical blessing' to the congregation: 'May the Lord bring you to the accomplishment of the Great Work, the

Summum Bonum, True Wisdom and Perfect Happiness.' It is interesting to note that this blessing is lifted bodily from the Adept Minor initiation ritual of the Golden Dawn.

The last composite occult group we wish to mention is one that illustrates the strand of 'modern witchcraft' in the rebirth of magic. We will call it the Aradia Coven – Aradia being one of the names of the goddess worshipped by the witches of today.

The origins of modern witchcraft and the beliefs and practices of those who rely on it for their spiritual nourishment are described later in this book. For the moment it suffices to say that while most of its devotees claim that their cult is of immemorial antiquity most outsiders who have taken an interest in the movement have come to the conclusion that it was largely the creation of Gerald Gardner, a retired customs officer whose interests included magic, flagellation and the collection of edged weapons.

It is easy enough to make fun of modern witchcraft, to remember such figures of fun as Peter Simple's Elvira Muttcliffe, the well known Sowerby Bridge *diseuse* who doubles as Witch Queen of the local coven, an eminently respectable group whose gatherings, sometimes attended by the Great Goat of Cleckheaton himself, feature no activities more sinister than the wearing of the trilby hat of invisibility and the serving of weak tea in bone china cups. But not all covens are so delightfully innocent. Some are positively criminal, and others serve as a means of satisfying their leaders' sexual lusts, often sado-masochistic in nature. It is only fair to add that most present-day covens are worthy, if eccentric, associations of pagans practising a perfectly legitimate nature worship. Still other groups, typified by our composite Aradia Coven, have more and more tended to concern themselves with herbal healing, astrology, and white magic rather than pure Gardnerian witchcraft and the (usually mild) bondage and flagellation practices associated with it.

Typically a coven such as Aradia began its life a quarter

of a century or less ago. Originally its members were remarkably ignorant of western occultism, taking everything written by such supposed experts on witchcraft as Margaret Murray and Gerald Gardner as holy writ. In time, however, the leaders of the coven came into contact with the teachings of such western esoteric teachers as, for example, Dion Fortune and Rudolf Steiner. Later on they made themselves acquainted with the standard literature of European magic, from the grimoires, the late medieval textbooks of ritual magic such as the *Key of Solomon*, to the *True Relation* of John Dee and the *Works* of Thomas Vaughan. Today the coven remains organised in the three degrees of modern witchcraft and still celebrates such traditional festivals as Lammas, Beltane and Midsummer – but the 'witchcraft' is in reality no more than an ossified framework supporting a secret society devoted to the study and practice of authentic ritual magic.

The three strands of modern ritual magic represented by our composite orders of 'the Secret Rose', 'Oz' and 'Aradia' are, of course, not the only ones, but they are the most important and influential and later on in this book we shall come upon them again and again.

But, one might ask, is it really *worth* bothering to study the beliefs and practices of the magicians, witches, alchemists who have been responsible for the rebirth of magic and other occult techniques which should, long ago, have been swept into that 'dustbin of history' to which Marxist journalists make such frequent reference? Surely there was, and still is, a large element of pure fraud in the behaviour of many of those most prominent in the European and American occult revival?

Certainly fraud exists, certainly charlatanism has been a characteristic of the most notable magicians of the last and present centuries; and yet, paradoxically, some of the worst charlatans have seemed to have something very like supernatural powers.

This strange combination of fraud, power and, sometimes, wisdom intrigued the novelist Gustav Meyrink, himself a student of the teachings of the Golden Dawn and an initiate of a Prague-based secret association known as the Blue Star. In his novel *Meister Leonhard* (1916) Meyrink described one of these ambivalent magicians, an occultist who called himself Dr. Schrepfer and

> . . . ate fire, swallowed swords, turned water into wine, thrust daggers through his cheek and tongue without drawing blood, healed possessed people, charmed away injuries, invoked spirits, bewitched men and cattle.
>
> Daily Leonhard realised that the man was a fraud who could neither read nor write yet performed wonders . . .
>
> Everything that the trickster said and did had a double aspect: he cheated men and at the same time helped them; he lied and his speech concealed the highest truth; he spoke the truth and the lie sneered forth. He fantasised carelessly and his words came true.

Christopher McIntosh has pointed out[2] that this passage conveys the fact that occult knowledge is often transmitted through seemingly disreputable channels, that a man can simultaneously be a cheap charlatan and a conveyer of the greatest wisdom. 'In fact,' adds Mr. McIntosh, 'it is hard to think of a great mystical teacher of recent times who did not have an element of the trickster or showman about him.'

But what, exactly, is the nature of the magic these 'tricksters' and 'showmen' teach and practice? What are the underlying beliefs, if any, what unite the devotees of occult rite and ceremony?

2 The Meaning of Magic

Late one evening, almost fifty years ago, William Gerhardie, an English novelist and playwright with little interest in occultism and no acquaintance at all with the literature of 'out of the body experiences', retired to sleep. He had not been drinking, was not a drug user, and was feeling no more than the 'nervous exhaustion' induced by a demanding work-schedule.

He awoke – so it seemed – from a dreamless slumber and sleepily groped for the switch of his bedside lamp. His seeking fingers found only a void and, surprised, he came to full consciousness. To his amazement he realised that his perceptions had been transferred to a sort of ghostly 'body' which was suspended, quite regardless of the law of physics, between the floor and ceiling of his bedroom. For some minutes he lay, like a captive balloon, where he was. Then he found himself settling unsteadily on his feet; he was never to be exactly sure how this happened – it felt, he said, rather as though he had been pushed.

By the dim light which filled the room and seemed to emanate from himself he groped his way towards the door and reached for the handle. But he could not grasp it. Somehow or other the muscles of his new body lacked all capacity to grip. Then he became conscious of the fact that a glowing coil – he described it as resembling 'the strong broad ray of dusty light at the back of a dark cinema projecting onto the screen in front' – was attached to him and led back to the bed on which he had been sleeping. There it lit the form of the sleeping body, his own physical self, to which it was connected.

At first Gerhardie was frightened by what was happening to him. Then curiosity overcame alarm and he decided to experiment with his new vehicle of consciousness. He found that while he could not open his bedroom door he could pass through it without difficulty. He moved into the bathroom, noting that its window was open and that a new towel rack had been installed, and then on into other rooms, carefully observing which windows were open and which shut. He passed through the front door and hovered, elated, in the air, feeling that he could *fly* anywhere he wished. His lightness of heart turned to anxiety. What would happen, he wondered, should the glowing cord connecting his new and old bodies be severed?

He flew back to his bed and looked down at his physical body. Then his courage was restored; 'not yet', he said to himself, and 'flew' away at great speed, his consciousness of his exact surroundings vanishing as he did so. He deliberately slowed down and found himself walking on a patch of grass. Looking behind him he saw that the cord had grown thin. With a jerk he found himself back in his usual body, still lying calmly abed.

Was the incident no more than a dream? No, decided Gerhardie, for there was '. . . quite another quality about it all, that of reality, which removed it from the mere memory of a dream. . . . I got up, and went through the rooms, checking the mental notes I had made about which windows were closed or open, which curtains drawn; and the evidence in all cases proved correct'.

Gerhardie's experience was unusual but by no means unique, for a surprising number of people have claimed spontaneous out-of-the-body experiences; and in 1968 Celia Green, of the Institute for Psychophysical Research, published an analysis of the testimonies of a group of 368 such people. Magicians and others concerned with the occult accept the objectivity of most of such experiences and explain them by saying that man has not just one body, the body in which we carry on our everyday lives, but several bodies; i.e. vehicles to which consciousness can be transferred. Similarly, while most magicians accept the reality of matter (and do not argue, like Christian Scientists and some Buddhists, that only spirit is real and all the rest illusion) they affirm that there are other forms of reality, other 'worlds' or 'planes', with their own modes of existence which, in certain circumstances, it is possible for human beings to experience.

Just how many there are of these planes and the human 'bodies' associated with them is a matter of opinion, or, perhaps, of the classification used – for while some occultists use a threefold, some a fivefold, and some a sevenfold system, all these are capable of reconciliation with one another.

Thus in the early writings of Dion Fortune, a magician and medium who has had great influence on the development of the western occult revival, the following divisions were used:

Human Entity	*Planes or Worlds*
1) Physical and Etheric Bodies	World of Matter (Assiah)
2) Lower Astral Body 3) Upper Astral Body	Astral World (Yetzirah)
4) Concrete Mental Body 5) Abstract Mental Body	Mind World (Briah)
6) Concrete Spiritual Body 7) Abstract Spiritual Body	Spiritual World (Atziluth)

The word in brackets following the names of the planes are English transliterations of Aramaic Chaldee terms used to describe the various types of reality supposedly emanating from Ain Soph Aur – 'God' in the purest sense of the word – in the mediaeval Jewish mystical system known as the qabalah. Almost all modern magicians consider themselves qabalists, and terms derived from the qabalah are widely used in European and American esoteric circles. It must be noted, however, that while aspects of the 'occult qabalah' are derived from the teachings of Jewish and Christian qabalists, occult qabalism is by no means identical with either the qabalah associated with mediaeval Judaism or the 'Christian qabalah' of the renaissance.

Of the other 'worlds' and 'bodies' it is those called 'astral' in which, as far as practical workings are concerned, western occultists are most interested. They believe that by manipulation of the 'stuff' that makes up the Astral ('Yetziratic') world – this 'stuff' was called Astral Light by the French magician Eliphas Lévi – they can influence both the physical universe and the feelings, thoughts, and modes of consciousness of themselves and other living beings.[1]

Magicians believe that out-of-the-body experiences of the type experienced by William Gerhardie involve the 'projection of the astral body' – i.e. its temporary separation from the physical body – and that by use of the appropriate magical techniques, capable of mastery by almost anyone, it is possible not only to carry out such projections at will but to visit any chosen 'country' of the astral world.

The projection techniques employed sometimes involve the use of drugs or hypnotism by an occult teacher, but such practices are – officially at any rate – frowned upon by most ritual magicians. The more usual method is to use what are called astral doorways, pictures or symbols seen both physically and in the mind's eye, as a means of autohypnosis.

An astral doorway is used as follows. The magician regards intently a chosen picture (for example, a tarot trump) or a symbol (for example, a red triangle or the black 'sigil' of a spirit) which supposedly has some relationship with the part of the astral world he or she 'wishes to visit' – that is the mode of consciousness designed to be experienced. After an unwandering attention has been achieved it is visually imagined that the object of contemplation enlarges itself to the size of a door.

This is comparatively easy; the next step is often found more difficult. The magician, holding the door in the mind's eye, and keeping the eyes closed, visualises it swinging open. The astral body, to which, by now, at least some part of consciousness should have been transferred, looks around at what lies beyond the doorway.

With determination and persistence it becomes possible, so it is averred, for consciousness to be fully transferred to the astral body which can then explore the astral kingdoms at will.

A number of magicians, past and present, have recorded such explorations in detail. Whether one believes that the new worlds described have some sort of objective reality, or whether one takes the reductionist view that they are merely aspects of the unconscious mind, there is no doubt that these accounts of astral heavens and hells make an appeal to all who appreciate good fantasy or – as the magicians would claim – *real* fantasy, fantastic reality.

Thus Florence Farr Emery, the late 19th century actress who combined an active love-life – Yeats and Shaw were amongst those she was emotionally involved with – with occult experimentation and ritual magic had some exciting astral experiences.

At some time in the 1890s she and a fellow magician named Elaine Simpson decided to undertake an astral journey to the sphere ruled by the goddess Venus. They used as their doorway the tarot trump called the Empress. This was because the hermetic order of which they were both initiates believed this card to have a symbolic relationship – a 'correspondence' – with all love goddesses and with the planet Venus in astrology.

They placed the trump before themselves, contemplated it and visualised it, as one of them later recorded, becoming 'spiritualised, heightened in colouring, purified in design and idealised'.

Then one or both of the seers chanted 'Daleth' – the name of the fourth letter of the Hebrew alphabet, supposed to qabalistically correspond to Venus and the chosen tarot card. They projected themselves through their doorway and saw a 'greenish blue distant landscape, suggestive of mediaeval tapestries'. Then they 'flew', forcing their bodies upwards through astral clouds. They found themselves in a 'pale green landscape' which sur-

The Rose Cross as conceived by the Golden Dawn and worn by its adepts (see p. 102) *Drawing by Miranda Payne.*

rounded 'a Gothic Temple of ghostly outlines marked in light'.

The women then approached the temple, finding that as they did so it gained in solidity. Giving the signs that showed that they had been initiated into the grade of their order which entitled them to explore the Venusian aspects of the astral plane, they entered the temple. They noted that opposite the entrance was a three-barred cross with a dove, a bird sacred to Venus perched upon it. Beside it were steps, which they descended into a gloomy passage. As they traversed it they met 'a beautiful green dragon', who meant no harm and moved on through the darkness. Eventually they emerged from their sombre surroundings to find themselves standing on a brilliantly white marble terrace.

Beyond the terrace they could see a flower garden, the leaves of the plants delicately green above and velvety white below. In the garden stood the astral figure – some aspect of Venus – which had been symbolised by the Empress of the Tarot. She was 'of heroic proportions, clothed in green with a jewelled girdle, a crown of stars on her head, in her hand a sceptre of gold, having at one apex lustrously white closed lotus flower; in her left hand an orb bearing a cross'.

The two occultists approached the being and enquired her name. Smilingly, she replied:

> I am the mighty Mother Isis; most powerful of all the world, I am she who fights not, but is always victorious. I am that Sleeping Beauty whom men have sought for all time. The paths which lead to my castle are beset with danger and illusions. Such as fail to find me, sleep; or may ever rush after the *Fata Morgana* leading astray all who feel that illusory influence. I am lifted up on high and draw men unto me. I am the world's desire, but few there be who find me. When my secret is told, it is the secret of the Holy Grail.

Then the 'Lady Venus' – for it was she who vivified the astral form beheld by the magicians – led them to a high turret where, so the goddess indicated, she would in some manner reveal to them the innermost nature of her mystery.

She began by showing them her secret under the veil of symbolism; they beheld a cup holding a ruby coloured fluid and the sun shining upon it. Then, in words, the goddess revealed to them – or so the occultists believed – the secret of the Holy Grail.

> . . . I have given my heart to the world, that is my strength. Love is the Mother of the Man-God, giving the quintessence of her life to save mankind from destruction, and to shew forth the path to eternal life. Love is the Mother of the Christ-Spirit, and this Christ is the highest love. Christ is the heart of love, the heart of the Great Mother Isis, the Isis of Nature. He is the expression of her power. She is the Holy Grail, and He is the life blood of Spirit that is found in the cup.

The women were impressed by this astral revelation. 'We solemnly gave our hearts,' recorded one of them, 'to the keeping of the Grail.' They then felt a great influx of courage and power, 'for our own hearts were henceforth to be in touch with hers, the strongest force in all the world.'

So ended the astral journey which, clearly enough, the two seers felt had been well worth undertaking. But the questions that remain to be answered are, firstly, whether the experience undergone was other than entirely subjective, and, secondly, whether any of the information conveyed was of real value or interest to the women who received it, or whether they had just indulged themselves by taking part in something very like a third-rate television adaptation of one of C.S. Lewis's Narnia stories.

To the first question there neither is, nor can be, any decisive answer. To the second one is at first inclined to answer with a flat negative. It does seem, however, that the declaration of the astral 'Lady Venus' is not without interest, in spite of the flowery and spuriously archaic language – reminiscent of the communications spewed out by a thousand Victorian trance mediums – in which it was delivered. Two points are of significance. The first is the identification of the Blessed Virgin, 'Mother of the Man-God', with Venus, goddess of love – that is, *sexual* love, *eros* not *agapé*. The second is the identification of the Grail, the sacred vessel of the Matter of Britain, with Venus, the archetypal *yoni* or female organ of generation.

The present-day reader, familiar with the symbol-interpretations of psycho-analysis, finds nothing surprising in the identification of a cup – even such a cup as that sought by Bors, Galahad and Parsifal – with the vagina; indeed, such an interpretation of the Grail legend has been familiar to students of Arthurian legend since the publication of Jessie L. Weston's *From Ritual to Romance* in 1911. Nevertheless it was an astonishing concept for two Victorian ladies spontaneously to light upon – for it is highly improbable that it was contained in any published source available to them nor was it part of the teaching of the magical group into which they had been initiated.

Even to the contemporary reader the other claim of the Lady Venus – that she must be identified with the 'Mother of the Christ-Spirit' – must seem odd, for it is difficult to reconcile the characters of the chaste Mary and the promiscuous Venus.

And yet similar links between the ever-virgin and the ever-erotic aspects of the feminine principle have been implicit in the teachings of some heretical sects. Thus the early leaders of the Mariavites, a Polish breakaway from Catholicism condemned by Pope Pius X as long ago as 1906 but still surviving in today's 'People's Democracy', believed their founder, a visionary nun named Maria Kozowska, to be an incarnation of the Virgin and yet four of them (all of whom were in course of time to receive a valid, though irregular, episcopal consecration) not only seem to have had sexual intercourse with her but to have considered this to have been the supreme religious experience of their lives.

Once again it seems to be impossible to believe that Mrs. Emery and Elaine Simpson, the two magicians whose astral jaunt we have been considering, could have had any literary source for their strange identification of virgin motherhood and promiscuity.

It seems at least possible that either they derived their intuitions from what Jungians call the Collective Unconscious or, even more unlikely, that they *did* journey to the realm of Venus and receive an authentic communication from an entity enjoying some sort of objective existence.

In the course of the astral journey which we have examined the seers were impressed by the symbols, colours and beings (e.g. a dove and a green dragon) which they saw. For these were, so they believed, 'in correspondence' with Venus and thus confirmed the validity of the experience.

The phrase 'in correspondence' relates to the 'doctrine of correspondences', one of the basic theoretical premises of western magicians past and present. The doctrine is perhaps the most difficult of magical theories for the modern westerner to understand and accept. For the ways of thinking, and the modes of observing the world around us that underlies the teaching are alien to, and at variance with, the concepts upon which all modern science is based.

Science sees the individual human being as a little bit – and, what is more, rather an unimportant little bit – of the universe. Magic asserts, in accordance with the doctrine of correspondences, that the individual *is* a universe which is an image of the greater universe which is around him.

From this it follows that every factor present in the human mind and soul is also present in the manifested universe and vice versa. Thus those factors in the make-up of a human being which are symbolically ruled by the goddess Venus – and, astrologically, the planet Venus – have an objective relationship (a *correspondence*) with all those plants, animals, geometric figures etc. which also fall under the dominion of Venus. Most of these correspondences appear fairly arbitrary to the non-occultist, but those magicians who have used them as a guide to the construction of rituals assert that they are effective. On the simplest level these correspondences can be used to induce mood changes; a choleric person can, for example, calm himself by avoiding the use of red, a colour corresponding with Mars, in the decoration of his home.

More complex ways of using the correspondences have frequently been employed. Thus in 1628 Pope Urban VIII, worried that an approaching eclipse of the sun was dangerous to him and might even indicate his forthcoming death, called on the magician Tomas Campanella for aid. Campanella prepared an 'astrological room', a symbolic solar system, for his client. Two large lamps symbolised sun and moon, and flaming torches the planets. The room was decorated in colours corresponding with Jupiter and Venus, considered beneficial planets by astrologers, and then furnished with plants, flowers, and even precious stones, believed to correspond to those planets. The Pope then sat in his little solar system, burning the incenses of Jupiter and Venus and listening to Jovial and Venereal music. As Richard Cavendish has remarked, it is likely that Pope and sorcerer were pleased with their efforts, for the former lived for another sixteen years.

Besides occult beliefs about the astral world and correspondences modern magicians attach great importance to theories concerning human willpower. The will, they assert, properly trained, and used in conjunction with faith and creative imagination, is capable of performing what seem to be miracles. It can transform the physical, emotional and spiritual capacities of both the magician and those he wishes to influence for good or ill. It can even produce physical alterations in the outside world; under certain circumstances it can even transmute base metals into gold.

There are various occult methods of training the will. One of the most popular with modern magicians is described as follows in one of the instructional documents of an occult fraternity:

> . . . imagine your head as a centre of attraction with thoughts like rays radiating out to a vast globe. To want or desire a thing is the first step in the exercise of Will; get a distinct image of the thing you desire, placed, as it

were, in your heart, concentrate all your wandering rays of thought upon this image until you feel it to be one glowing scarlet ball of compacted force. Then project this concentrated force on the subject you wish to affect.

It will be noted that this exercise involves the use of both willpower and the visual imagination, and a paper circulated in the same fraternity emphasised the indivisibility of the two in effective magical workings.

> To practise magic both the Imagination and the Will must be called into action, they are co-equal in the work . . . the Imagination must precede the Will in order to produce the greatest possible effect.
>
> The Will unaided can send forth a current, and that current cannot be wholly inoperative, yet its effect is vague and indefinite. . . . The Imagination unaided can create an image . . . yet it can do nothing of importance, unless vitalised and directed by the Will.
>
> When, however, the two are conjoined, when the Imagination creates an image and the Will directs and uses that image, marvellous magical effects may be obtained.

As well as such beliefs as those outlined above a major influence on the activities of those concerned in the rebirth of magic has been exerted by the strange occult texts known as the grimoires.

3 Grimoires and Sorcerers

Almost everyone who enjoys supernatural fiction is familiar with the tales of occult horror written by H.P. Lovecraft and his many imitators. Many of these stories show a remarkable similarity of plot.

A young man, scholarly and introverted, acquires a copy of a mysterious book, usually by inheriting it from an ancestor of sinister reputation or by coming across it on the shelves of an obscure bookshop. The book – sometimes Ludwig Prinn's *Mysteries of the Worm*, sometimes Von Junzt's *Unspeakable Cults*, more usually the *Necronomicon* of 'the mad Arab, Abdul Alhazred' – fascinates its new owner. He sees less and less of his friends and begins instead to haunt old libraries, cult meeting-places and burial grounds. He talks wildly of certain 'Great Old Ones'. He seeks the company of the debased inhabitants, usually froglike in appearance, of decaying New England seaports. Finally he meets with an unpleasantness which ends his interest in books and ours in him. He is struck by lightning. Or turns into an amphibian. Or is carried off into 'alien dimensions' by the 'Great Old Ones' – updated versions of devils and demons. If unusually lucky he is removed, raving wildly, to a padded cell, there to spend the rest of his days.

All the forbidden books mentioned above were non-existent at the time the stories about them were written, although in recent years, as will be described in a later chapter, several spoof *Necronomicons* have been produced. Nevertheless, these imaginary books are a fictional reflection of a certain reality – of a literature that has existed for over two thousand years. The study of this literature may or may not have resulted in anyone being carried off by devils, but it has led, and still leads, some of those who have devoted themselves to it into strange and dangerous places, stranger and more dangerous activities, curious lives and even more curious deaths.

The literature in question is that of the grimoires, magical cookbooks purporting to teach their users how to obtain all they desire – usually power, love, money, or some combination of these – by means of occult ceremony. 'Grimoire' means no more than 'grammar'. Mystic phrases were (and are) considered of such importance in Western magic that the Middle English word 'grammarye' meant 'magic' as well as 'grammar' in the modern sense of the word.

Exactly how early in time grimoires were first compiled is uncertain; certainly there were textbooks of magic in ancient Egypt and Babylonia. But the grimoires of mediaeval and renaissance Europe (for it is these that have exerted a powerful influence on the modern rebirth of magic) seem to have been Christianised descendants of largely Jewish magical works which were widely circulated in the Hellenistic world of the Eastern Mediterranean during the first few centuries of the Christian era.

Many of these books were attributed to King Solomon who, according to legend, had magic powers which gave him dominion over angels, demons and men. The *Testament of Solomon*, a Greek manuscript probably dating from the third century A.D., gave a catalogue of demons (the names of which were derived from a medley of Hebrew, Greek, Coptic and even Persian) and listed the 'Names of Power' which were believed to control them. A later work, the *Sword of Moses*, not only showed mingling of Jewish and Graeco-Egyptian influences but betrayed the theological and moral confusion of those who compiled and used it as a working textbook. For the most holy Divine Names were employed in the composition of spells designed to achieve such diverse ends as striking an enemy blind, forcing a woman's chastity and sending a neighbour unpleasant dreams.

The most widespread of the mediaeval grimoires was the *Key of Solomon*. While almost all surviving manuscripts of this grimoire date from no earlier than the 15th century, it seems probable that they are late variants of Greek originals a thousand years older and perhaps transmitted to the Latin culture of Western Europe after the Venetians had looted Greek-speaking Constantinople in 1204. It may well be significant that the oldest copy of the *Key* in the British Library is in Greek and probably dates from the latter half of the 12th century.

The Solomonic family of grimoires show the same moral ambivalence as earlier magical texts. On the one hand they employ Divine and Angelic Names in their conjurations, instruct the magician to recite lengthy passages from the Old Testament, particularly the Psalms of David, and tell how the sign of the cross should be used as a protection against evil spirits. On the other hand the ends intended to be achieved by the use of the Solomonic formulae are usually less than admirable. They vary from the merely greedy (the finding of hidden treasure and successful gambling) to the silly and futile (such as 'hindering a sportsman from killing any game'); from the mild lechery of spells designed to gain love to the jealousy enshrined in the following instruction for 'experiments upon enemies' – a rite designed to create discord between lovers.

> Experiments upon enemies may be performed in several ways, but whether with waxen images or some other instrument, the particulars of each must be diligently and faithfully observed. . . . recite the following words once over the same image:- "VSOR, DILIPIDATORE, TENTATORE, SOIGNATORE, DEVORATORE, CONCITORE ET SEDUCTORE. O, all ye ministers and companions, I direct, conjure, constrain and command ye to fulfil this behest willingly . . . that as the face of the one is contrary to the other, so the same may never look more upon one another." Deposit the image in some place

> perfumed with evil odours, especially those of Mars, such as sulphur. . . . Let it remain there for one night, having duly asperged it, observing the proper hour and time.

This spell is common-sense itself when compared with an 'experiment' to be found in the *Grimorium Verum*, a late derivative of the Solomonic texts subtitled 'the Most Approved Keys of Solomon the Hebrew Rabbin'. The process in question supposedly enables its user to obtain truthful answers to questions on 'any art or science', to learn details of any buried treasures concealed nearby, and – perhaps most desired by those who have tried the spell – to gain possession of a ring which 'worn on the finger, will render you lucky at play, while if it be placed upon the finger of any woman or girl, you shall there and then have your delight with them'. The rite in question is described simply enough:

> After supper pass in secret to your chamber . . . kindle a good fire. Place a white cloth on the table, round which set three chairs, and before each chair, upon the table, let there be a wheaten roll and a glass full of fresh clear water. Lastly, draw up a couch and a chair to the side of the bed, and retire to rest, uttering the following conjuration: "Besticitum consalatio veni ad me vertat Creon, Creon, Creon, cantor laudem omnipotentis et non commentur. Stat superior carta vient laudem omviestra principiem da montem et inimicos meas o protantis vobis et mihi dantes que passium fieri sincisibus."

The results of this will be immediate, claimed the author of the grimoire. Three persons will arrive through the window of the chamber and

> will rest themselves near the fire . . . finally thanking him or her who has entertained them. . . . The said three persons will draw lots amongst one another to know which of them shall remain with you. If a man be the operator, she who wins will place herself in the arm-chair which you have set by the bed, and she will remain

> and commune with you until midnight, at which hour she will depart with her companions, without any need of dismissal. . . . So long as she remains you may question her upon any art or science, or upon any subject whatsoever, and she will immediately give you a positive answer. You may also enquire of her whether she is aware of any hidden treasure, and she will instruct you as to its locality and the precise time suited to its removal. She will even appear there with her companions to defend you. . . . At parting, she will present you with a ring. . . .

The real core of the grimoires is concerned with the raising, to visible appearance, of infernal and supernal spirits with the object of obtaining benefits from them. Such supposed benefits are sometimes crudely material – gold or sex – sometimes more intellectual: a 'knowledge of hidden sciences', for example. The exact processes laid down differ from grimoire to grimoire, but the fundamental stages are the same. Firstly, the preparation of all the material substances and occult implements to be used in the ceremony. Secondly the purification of the body and soul of the magician and, finally, the actual performance of the rite.

The first stage is in many ways the most difficult, and some modern participants in the 'rebirth of magic' who have experimented with the grimoires have been reduced to near-despair by the difficulty of complying with all the things demanded of them. The experimenter has to compound his own incense, to manufacture his own beeswax or tallow candles, to make parchment out of animal skins. He has to blend his own ink – compounded of gum, soot, water and oak galls – and use it to write out his ritual on parchment. He has to manufacture and consecrate 'magical weapons', amongst them a wand, a sword, two knives and a sickle. These must be made at particular times, when the astrological conditions are suitable, and then subjected to weird processes. The sickle, for example, has to be forged from a piece of new steel during the first hour after sunrise on the day of Mercury (Wednesday).

Then it has to be given a white boxwood handle. After this the blade must be thrice heated to redness and then tempered in a mixture of herbal juices mixed with magpie's blood.

Although the magician does not have to submit himself to processes quite so drastic as this, the rites of self-purification and consecration are almost as complicated. One early text lays down that the experimenter must first be chaste for seven days ending on the third day after the New Moon. On that day he must go, before dawn, to a river bank and there build a stone altar. At the moment of sunrise he should decapitate a white cockerel, throw its head into the river, and drink the bird's blood. He must then burn the carcase on an olivewood fire, jump into the river, climb out backwards, put on new clothes and, finally, walk away without looking behind him.

Not all preparatory exercises are so physically energetic, nor do they involve blood sacrifice. *The Sworn Book of Honorius*, the most authentically Christian of all the grimoires, gives instructions which are both morally above reproach and easy to follow:

> Be penitent and truly confessed of all sins, forbearing . . . all female enticements . . . for Solomon saith "it is better to live with a bear or lion in its den than live with a wicked woman". You may not keep company with sinful or wicked men, for David saith "with the wicked you will be wicked and with the holy you will be holy". Therefore you must lead a pure and clean life, for David saith "blessed are the undefiled and those that walk in the Law of the Lord". Let not your clothes be filthy, but new or well washed; Solomon means by new garments virtue and a pure life, for God and his Angels care neither for wordly things nor for appearances. For a poor man doth sooner work affectively in this art than a rich one, but clean vestments are necessary, for Angels live with God are clean and thus desire communication with clean men only. Be never idle lest you be inclined to sin . . . and always pray to God with the following prayers . . .

LES CLAVICULES DE SALOMON

Traduit de l'Hébreux en Langue Latine,
Par le Rabin Abognazar,

ET

Mis en langue Vulgaire Par M. BARAULT Archevêque d'Arles.

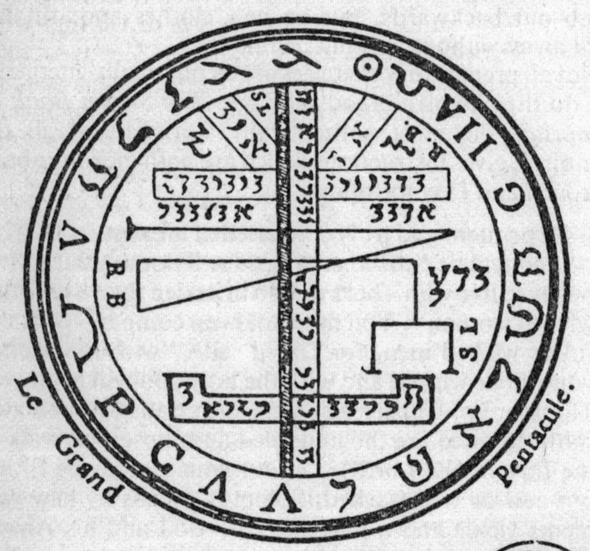

M. DC. XXXIV.

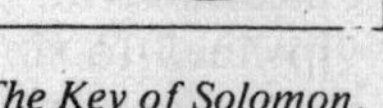

Frontispiece of a seventeenth-century version of *The Key of Solomon*.

There follows a demanding schedule of daily devotions – nine a day on the first four days of the week, twenty-six a day on Fridays, Saturdays and Sundays. These prayers blend orthodox piety with the long strings of usually meaningless syllables termed 'the barbarous words of evocation'. The following is typical:

> O Most High and Invisible God . . . by Thy most holy angels . . . I humbly beseech you . . . deihel depimo dewhel excludo depimon helinon exmogon . . . illuminate and confirm my understanding with the sweetness of Thy Holy Spirit . . .

Having manufactured his implements and consecrated both them and himself the magician can then proceed to the actual evocation of demons. He stands within a triple circle inscribed with names and symbols. This is essential for his own protection; should a demon be able to reach him it would tear him in pieces. He then burns an incense appropriate to the spirit whose presence he requires. Most of the grimoires give classified lists of spirits and the incenses which should be used for them. These frequently contradict one another. Thus the *Sworn Book of Honorius* recommends for martial spirits an incense compounded of euphorbium, bedellium, gum ammoniac, roots of black and white hellebore, powdered lodestone and sulphur. This, instructs the grimoire, should be mixed to a paste with 'human blood, the blood of a black cat, and the brain of a raven'. For the same spirits the *Magical Elements* of Peter de Abano prescribes the simplest of all incenses – burning pepper.

The magician recites his conjurations – the actual spells that command the appearance of the demon. Those laid down in the *Goetia* – according to Aleister Crowley by far the most efficacious contained in any grimoire save that of Abra-Melin – are typical. There is a first conjuration which the operator is instructed to repeat 'as often as thou pleasest'; if the spirit does not respond the second conjuration is to be used. Should this also be unsuccessful the *Goetia* gives a further spell called the Constraint. If this does not produce the desired appearance:

> . . . thou mayest be sure that he is sent unto some other place by his King, and he cannot come; and if it be so, invocate the King as here followeth, to send him. But if he do not come still, then thou mayest be sure that he is bound in chains in hell, and that he is not in the custody of his King. If so, and thou still hast a desire to call him even from thence, thou must recite the general curse which is called the Spirits' Chain.

It is clear that even this sometimes failed, for the author of the *Goetia* suggests a further procedure.

> . . . write thou his seal on parchment and put thou it into a strong black box; with brimstone, asafoetida, and such like things that bear a stinking smell; and then bind the box up round with an iron wire, and hang it upon the point of thy sword, and hold it over the fire of charcoal . . .

If after this, and the recital of a 'fire Conjuration', the spirit still proves obstinate the magician solemnly curses it:

> . . . since thou art still pernicious and disobedient, and wilt not appear unto me to answer . . . I do . . . curse thee, and deprive thee of all thine office, joy, and place; and I do bind thee in the depths of the Bottomless Abyss there to remain until the Day of Judgement, I say into the Lake of Fire and Brimstone which is prepared for all rebellious, disobedient and obstinate, and pernicious spirits . . . And as thy name and seal contained in this box chained and bound up, shall be choken in sulphurous stinking substances, and burned in this material fire so . . . I do cast thee . . . into the Lake of Fire . . . there to remain unto the day of doom . . .
>
> Then the exorcist must put the box into the fire and by-and-by the spirit will come, but as soon as he is come, quench the fire that the box is in, and make a sweet perfume, and give him welcome and a kind entertainment . . .
>
> Then he or they will be obedient, and bid thee ask

> what thou wilt, for he or they be subjected by God to fulfil our desires and commands. . . .

On the face of it many of the processes outlined in the grimoires are absurd and/or disgusting; few of us would have the heart to use the blood of animals to compound our incenses and some of the material substances that the magician is urged to use in his spells can only be obtained by engaging in a number of unpleasant activities. Many modern occultists have therefore denied that the processes outlined in the grimoires are intended to be followed literally; they should, such occultists affirm, be interpreted symbolically. Thus, for example, one 18th century grimoire instructs the magician who wants to inflict a sleepless night on his enemy to 'pick a June lily under the waning moon, soak it in laurel juice and bury it in dung; worms will breed therein, dry them and scatter on the enemy's pillow.' This means, it is said, invokes the demons Lilith (the June lily) and Q'areb Zarag (the laurel). Similarly a spell involving the use of a toad or its organic products must be interpreted as instructing the magician to evoke Bilifares, a toad-headed demon.

In any case, not all the techniques described in the grimoires are in themselves repellent. Nor are all the ends these same occult experiments are designed to achieve, silly, greedy, or lecherous. The *Sworn Book of Honorius* gives a method of magically obtaining the Beatific Vision – the goal of mystics of all ages.

The magician begins this process by a month-long period of preparation; he prays, goes on to a diet of bread and water, attends Mass and takes communion. He then makes a sleeping couch of exorcised hay and surrounds it with ashes and a magic circle around which are written the Hundred Names of God. After a ceremonial washing in spring water he dons a hair shirt and black vestments and recites a prayer:

> 'Zabuather Rabumae . . . Orka which þe Gabriel in the Temple . . . Christus who did show thyself without spot . . . Hospesk who made the dry rod flourish . . .

> Gofgar . . . Occynnomos who did send the first star to the Three Kings . . . Elvorem . . . Theloy who at Cana turned water into wine . . . Archima who for 32 years did preach . . . the Catholic faith . . . Rabuch . . . Look upon me and hearken to my prayers: that . . . thou wouldst vouchsafe to deliver my soul from the darkness of my body and filthiness of my sins, for in thee do I end my life O My God, Stoexkor, Abalay, Scyystalgaona, Fullarite, Reshphiomoma, Remiare, Baceda, Canona, Onlepot, Who said on the Cross *Consummatum Est'*.Then sleep and say no more, and you shall see the Celestial Palace, and the Majesty of God in His Glory, and the Nine Choirs of Angels, and the Company of all blessed spirits.

One grimoire stands out from all the others, *The Sacred Magic of Abra-Melin the Mage*, a work which claims to have been written in 1458 but which, in the form in which it has survived, is unlikely to date from earlier than the eighteenth century. The *Sacred Magic* describes a technique which is more akin to the Bhakta-Yoga of India than to the dramatic ceremonial processes of European magic.

The magician has to retire from the world and embark upon a six-month long retreat. This period is a sort of occult gestation, for at the end of the time the magician is, in a sense, born again; he gains what the grimoire calls 'the Knowledge and Conversation of the Holy Guardian Angel'. From the wording of the grimoire it would seem that this 'Knowledge and Conversation' is to be understood literally, the magician is to become acquainted with his Holy Guardian Angel in the same way that he has, in the past, become acquainted with his friends. Modern students of Abra-Melin, however, have argued that the phrase is to be interpreted symbolically. By the 'Knowledge and Conversation of the Holy Guardian Angel', they affirm, is meant a mystical process which can be more accurately referred to as 'the Union of the Higher and Lower Selves', or as the 'Union of Subject and Object', or as 'Cosmic Consciousness', or even – for those who like the terminology of Jungian psychology – as 'individuation'.

After the spiritual exercises to which the magician must devote most of the retreat have been carried out, and the 'Knowledge and Conversation' achieved, the Abra-Melin squares may be used. These are simple lettered, or partly lettered squares which the magician can employ for many curious purposes. Thus, for example, the squares below are supposed to enable the user to 'take possession of a great treasure' (left-hand square) and to 'cause hail' (right-hand square).

S	E	G	I	L	A	H
E	R	A	L	I	P	A
G						
I	L	E	N	L	I	
L						
A						
H						

C	A	N	A	M	A	L
A	M	A	D	A	M	A
N	A	D	A	D	A	M
A	D	A	N	A	D	A
M	A	D	A	D	A	N
A	M	A	D	A	M	A
L	A	M	A	N	A	C

It is interesting to note that although Aleister Crowley always carried about him a piece of parchment lettered with the left-hand square he never succeeded, in the literal sense of the words, in finding 'a great treasure'. After his death the talisman found its way into the possession of an ex-disciple who, only half-seriously, used it to find the 'great treasures' of rare occult books. He was most successful in this. . . . Segilah, the keyword of this square, is probably an Aramaic Chaldee word meaning simply 'treasure', while Canamal, the keyword of the right-hand square is probably a derivation of the Hebrew word ChNML, meaning large hailstones.

For the sake of any readers who may be tempted to experiment with the squares we had better add that the attempted use of them is supposedly extremely dangerous to anyone who has not achieved the Knowledge and Conversation of the Holy Guardian Angel and that – in the words of S.L. MacGregor Mathers – certain squares have 'a dangerous automatic nature . . . for, if left carelessly about, they are very liable to obsess sensitive persons, children, and even animals'.

According to occult report the composer 'Peter Warlock' must be numbered amongst those who have fallen a victim to the Abra-Melin squares. Desperately desiring a certain event he had the appropriate square tattooed on his arm and energized it – that is, kept his mind continually concentrated upon it – by blistering the tattooed skin with the glowing end of a cigarette. He obtained his desire, but in such a fashion that the event was an emotional disaster rather than a triumph, and he immediately committed suicide.

Whether or not animals can be obsessed by lettered squares, and whether or not one incurs any perils, save those of hepatitis acquired from dirty needles by having magical symbols tattooed upon one's body, there is no doubt that those who have experimented with the techniques of the grimoires have sometimes had cause to regret it. Such unfortunates may broadly be divided into three categories. The first consists of magicians who came to their ends in such notorious circumstances that it is impossible to disentangle fact from fantasy in the surviving accounts of their lives. The second group consists of men born in humble circumstances who have tried to use the magic of the grimoires as an escape from the tedium of their everyday lives. The final category consists of occultists who have used their supposed powers to gain influence over others and have been eventually destroyed by the jealousies and fears they have aroused.

The best-known example of an occultist of the first sort, one whose supposed biography combines fact with myth and legend, is Dr. Faustus. A similar magician, one to whom Crowley referred in his novel *Moonchild*, was Antony of Prague, who supposedly flourished in the early 15th century. Antony had

> made a Pact with the Demon, and had given himself over to him in body and in soul . . . the deceitful Leviathan had promised him forty years of life to do his pleasure. . . .
>
> He rendered himself invisible, he used to fly in the air, he used to enter through the keyholes into locked-

up rooms. . . . Ultimately his body was found dragged through the streets, and his head without any tongue therein, lying in a drain. And this was all the profit he drew from his Diabolical Science and Magic.

A magician who typifies the third category, and who was also 'dragged through the streets', was Dr. John Lamb, the occult adviser of James I's favourite, the Duke of Buckingham.

Lamb, whose date of birth is unknown, first came into notoriety in 1608 when he was charged with having used 'execrable arts to consume the body and strength of Thomas, Lord Windsor'. He was found guilty but never sentenced – presumably he already had powerful protectors – and a few months later he was again in court, this time accused of evoking 'evil and impious spirits'. This time he was imprisoned. At first in Worcester Castle, and then in the King's Bench, London. The transfer took place at the request of the inhabitants of Worcester; they were convinced that Lamb was still working evil magic, for after his conviction 'the High Sheriff, Foreman of Jury, and divers others . . . then present . . . died within a fortnight'.

Lamb's mysterious protectors ensured that his imprisonment was, although lengthy, of little inconvenience to him. He seems to have had several rooms at his disposal, to have had the best of food and drink at his table, and to have been able to entertain friends and clients. He even had serving wenches; in 1623 he was charged with raping one of these, an eleven year old girl, to whom he gave a venereal infection. He was found guilty but pardoned by James I and released from confinement. Probably this was due to the intervention of Buckingham, a client of his who seems to have had enormous confidence in Lamb's magical powers.

The reputation of the sorcerer was now considerable, the citizens of London regarding him with a mixture of fear and loathing. So great was his notoriety as a master of black magic that when an exceptionally powerful storm caused much damage in June 1626, this storm being accompanied by a sinister Thames fog through which some claimed to have seen dim and awful figures moving, it was widely assumed that Lamb was responsible.

By early 1628 Lamb's unpopularity reached its height. He had become looked upon as Buckingham's 'devil' and street ballads accused him of casting spells which brought chaste women to his patron's bed.

Finally, in 1628, Lamb was dragged and beaten through the streets by a mob of apprentices, dying the next morning. A crystal ball and other magical implements were found upon his body.

Two months later Buckingham was assassinated. The popular assumption attributed the success of the murderer to the cessation of Lamb's occult protection – in the words of a ballad:

> The Shepherd's struck, the sheep are fled,
> For want of Lamb, the Wolf is dead.

As for the humbler sorcerers, the men who employed grimoire magic with the aim of self-advancement, of most of them we can know little. They lived, evoked demons, and died in obscurity. But there are records of a few of them – of, for example, young Thomas Parkes, who practised magic in the last decade of the 17th century with the aid of the *Fourth Book of Occult Philosophy* attributed to Cornelius Agrippa. His first experiment in evocation raised spirits 'in the shape of little girls, about a foot and a half high'. Parkes, emboldened by his success, decided to go further and to acquire a 'familiar spirit'. He believed he had succeeded in this, claiming to have a familiar whom he called Malachi. Then, one December, he carried out a rite as the result of which spirits

> appeared faster than he wished them, and in most dreadful shapes – like serpents, lions, bears, etc., hissing at him, which did very much affright him; and the more so when he found it was not in his power to lay them, expecting every moment to be torn in pieces . . . and from that time he was never well so long as he lived. . . .

The occultists of modern times, the men and women who have brought about the rebirth of magic, have, as has been said, a more romantic, symbolic interpretation of the grimoires than such predecessors as Dr. Lamb and Thomas Parkes. This new interpretation had its origins in the French occult revival which began in the second half of the last century.

4 *The French Occult Revival*

At some time in 1854 a Frenchman who was enjoying a lengthy visit to England stood alone in a curiously furnished London room. In the centre of the room was a white marble altar inscribed with a pentagram and circled by a magnetized iron chain. Upon the altar was a copper chafing-dish, another stood upon a tripod, and on each wall was a large concave mirror.

The appearance of the man was as unusual as his surroundings. He wore white vestments, was crowned with a wreath of vervain entwined with a golden chain, and carried a sword. He was about to begin the 'evocation to visible appearance' – in other words the inducement of a spirit to appear in bodily form – of the ghost of Apollonius of Tyana, a Pythagorean teacher and wonder-worker of the lst century A.D. whose supposed feats, which included driving disease away from Ephesus, descending into Hades, and revealing a young bride as a vampire[1], have fascinated magicians for almost two thousand years.

The would-be evoker was Alphonse Louis Constant, better known to posterity by his pseudonym of Eliphas Lévi. He had been born in 1810, the son of a poor cobbler. His earliest years were spent in bitter poverty, but he was an intelligent child, described as 'eating books', and he managed to escape from his environment by the traditional route of the Catholic poor: finding that he had a vocation for the priesthood and thus obtaining a free seminary education.

While his discovery of his supposed vocation was a convenient one there is no reason to doubt his real piety and belief as a boy and a young man. In later life he described his feelings at his first communion:

> Through the mysteries of Catholicism I caught a glimpse of the infinite. My heart became impassioned towards a God who sacrificed himself for his children and transformed himself into bread in order to nourish them. The gentle figure of the sacrificed Lamb made me shed tears and the tender Name of Mary made my heart palpitate.

Although Lévi found no difficulty in reaching the academic standards demanded by his superiors he disliked both his first seminary and the more advanced one, Saint-Sulpice, which he entered in 1832. Writing of the latter he said:

> The *Sulpiciens* are cold and monotonous men for whom . . . regulations and . . . theological textbooks take the place of spirit and emotion. Custom is everything with them. Progress is a word that is considered profane and ridiculous. Art and poetry are regarded as childish and dangerous . . . A little memory to retain ancient scholastic arguments, a little subtlety to adapt them to modern Gallic fashions, a little volubility to enunciate them and twist their tails round reason – these are the qualities that pass for talent at Saint-Sulpice. Add to this a stiff manner, oily skin, greasy hair, a revolting cassock, dirty hands and shifty eyes and you have the full picture of what is called a good subject . . .

Lévi became a deacon, retaining his faith in spite of his dislike for his teachers and associates, but was never ordained to the priesthood, for he came to the conclusion that celibacy was not for him, feeling, as he put it, 'an imperious need for love', and deciding that he could not take vows 'before the altar of a cold and egotistical cult without remorse'.

Lévi left Saint-Sulpice in 1836. Three years or so later he

came into contact with 'strange doctrines' as the result of his friendship with Alphonse Esquiros, an early decadent whose mannered novel, *The Magician*, is described as including amongst its characters a harem of zombies, a brazen robot which tiresomely and incessantly preached the virtues of chastity, and a hermaphrodite who carried on a correspondence with the spirit of the moon. The doctrines in question were those of Ganneau, a half-mad royalist, a tattered, garret-inhabiting prophet who believed himself to be a reincarnation of Louis XVII. Years later, in his *History of Magic*, Lévi was to give an amusing and detached account of the antics of Ganneau and his wife, the latter supposedly a reincarnation of Marie Antoinette. At the time, however, his attitude was far from detached, for Ganneau's eloquence overcame Lévi's imagination, the failed priest becoming an enthusiastic advocate of the pseudo-Messiah's blend of unorthodox religion, royalism and utopian socialism. In fairness to Lévi it must be stated that he was by no means the only one to have all intellectual resistance swept away by Ganneau's burning belief in himself, his doctrines and his mystical powers; another of the prophet's disciples was the pioneer feminist Flora Tristan, whose grandson, the painter Gauguin, described his forebear as 'a socialist and an anarchist . . . credited with having founded . . . a certain religion . . . the religion of Mapa . . .'

Eventually Lévi decided that Ganneau was a false prophet, but before he did so he wrote a socialistic-cum-mystic book *The Bible of Liberty*, published in 1841, which earned him an eight-month prison sentence for blasphemy and subversion. After his release he supported himself by tutoring and hack writing, producing a whole volume of the *Dictionary of the Christian Religion* and a treatise on the Virgin sufficiently heterodox for at least one French bishop to forbid his flock to read it.

In 1852 Lévi met Hoene Wronski, a 74-year-old naturalised Frenchman who had been born a Pole, who had spent much time in attempts to reconcile science, occultism and religion, who believed that he had discovered the 'secret of the Absolute', who attempted to produce perpetual motion, and who had constructed the prognometer, a machine for producing predictions which, from its description, would seem to have been a mechanical adaptation of a simple device invented by Ramon Lull some five hundred years earlier[2].

Lévi already had a nodding acquaintance with occultism. As a seminarian one of his teachers had introduced him to animal magnetism (i.e. primitive, and occultly inclined, hypnotism), and his wide reading had included the more easily available mystical treatises, some of them of doubtful orthodoxy, and while in prison he had studied the writings of Swedenborg, the 18th century mystic and psychic whose teachings had influenced such dissimilar writers as Blake and Balzac. Contact with

Eliphas Lévi's version of the 'Trident of Paracelsus' (see page 54).

Wronski transformed Lévi's vague interests into a burning enthusiasm. He voraciously read occult literature, rapidly acquiring a wide but shallow knowledge of the subject.

Soon he came to believe that he understood the qabalah, that he had unlocked the mysteries that lay concealed in the obscurities of such authors as Postel, Basil Valentine, and Paracelsus, that he could provide the explanation of all the phenomena of spiritualism and mesmerism, and that the secrets magic, alchemy and esoteric symbolism were all within his grasp.

Lévi decided to make his discoveries known to the world and produced *The Dogma and Ritual of High Magic*, shown by internal evidence to have been conceived as one work although the *Dogma* and the *Ritual* were published separately, the former in 1854, the latter two years later. There is no doubt that in these books, as in his later productions, Lévi treated what he knew of the theory, practice and history of magic and alchemy in an extremely cavalier way, being only too ready to engage in deliberate distortion if he thought it would make good copy.

Take, for example, the 'Trident of Paracelsus', a drawing of which, showing a three-pronged fork inscribed with various names and symbols, illustrates the *Ritual*. After identifying the three prongs with, firstly, the Trinity, and secondly, the alchemical principles of Salt, Sulphur and Mercury, Lévi stated that:

> This trident is a pantacle expressing the synthesis of the triad in the monad, thus completing the sacred tetrad. He (Paracelsus) ascribed to this figure all the virtues which kabalistic Hebrews attribute to the name of Jehovah and the thaumaturgic properties of ABRACADABRA, used by the hierophants of Alexandria. Let us recognize here that it is a pantacle and consequently a concrete and an absolute sign of an entire doctrine, which has been that of an immense magnetic circle, not only for ancient philosophers but also for adepts of the Middle Ages . . .

Now it is certainly true that this trident was written of

with approval by Paracelsus; an illustration of it together with a description of its amazing powers appeared in the *Archidoxes Magicae* which was included in the *Collected Works* of Paracelsus edited by John Huser. On the other hand Paracelsus neither attributed to it all the virtues of the name Jehovah nor claimed that it symbolised Father, Son and Holy Spirit. He regarded it as a useful implement for the cure of sexual impotence generated by witchcraft, writing:

> The loss of Strength and Virtue in the Members of Generation is a certain Sympathy proceeding from gross Fatness, which as a certain *Spasma* impedites the power of the Members of that place. This happens by divers accidents; some whereof are natural, others are against nature, by Witchcraft . . . when it happens that this disease is brought upon any one by Witchcraft, or some Diabolical Art, wrought by the malice of wicked people: let the Patient take a piece of Horse-shoe found in the highway, of which let there be made a Trident-Fork on the day of Venus (Friday), and hour of Saturn . . . let those words with their Characters be engraven . . . on Sunday before Sun-rising; which being done, let the Fork be fastened in the ground under a running Stream of Water, so deep, that the handle may not be seen, and that it cannot be found: by this means, thou shalt be delivered in 9 days; and the person that has brought this mischief upon thee, shall get something himself in that place, from which he shall not so easily be delivered . . . [3]

Lévi's distortion of Paracelsus – so gross that it must be considered a deliberate mystification rather than a piece of carelessness – was typical of the way in which he misused occult sources to bolster up his own theories, reputation, and dogmas. Thus he chose to believe that the tarot cards were of enormous antiquity and contained profound qabalistic symbols. As there were no occult associations with the tarot before the last twenty years of the eighteenth century Lévi was forced to invent them, boldly stating that there were references to the mysterious cards in the writings of such men as Abbot Trithemius, the 16th century cryptographer and scholar, and Knorr von Rosenroth, the 17th century Christian qabalist. In reality no such references are to be found; and for reliable accounts of Western occult history and traditions one has to look elsewhere than in the works of Eliphas Lévi. This has led many, particularly those with little sympathy for occult pretensions, to take a poor view of the magical writings of the French mage. Professor Dummett, for example, has characterized them 'as the product of an advanced state of intellectual delinquescence', remarked that in them 'the centuries blend and blur . . . indeed everything blends and blurs', and asserted that they were 'designed to appeal to those who wanted religiosity without religion, who hankered after the bizarre and arcane and were flattered to think themselves the heirs of a secret and ancient wisdom of which the world at large remained ignorant . . .'

These criticisms are harsh but perhaps not altogether unjustified. It must always be remembered, however, that Lévi lived by his writings, that he had to meet the demands of his market if he was to eat and drink; he could simply not afford to spend his time producing, say, scholarly studies of the development of textual criticism. Admittedly Lévi romanticized the magical and alchemical traditions and what little he knew of the qabalah and other forms of Jewish mysticism – but it is a mistake to underestimate him, to see him as no more than a vulgarizer, tongue firmly in cheek, using the hermetic tradition as foundation on which to build an extravagant folly of fantasy and extravagant speculation. For he genuinely seems to have believed that in his writings on the 'Astral Light' he had supplied a rational explanation for all supposedly supernatural mediumship. Equally, he felt that the claims he made for the validity of his personal interpretation of occult tradition were justified. Magic, he averred, was of great value when it was properly understood, and, under the veils of a concealing symbolism, its doctrines expressed ultimate truths about good and evil, about wisdom, love and power. Indeed, for Lévi, magic, in the highest sense, was the only universally valid religion, the inner body of truth that was the heart and marrow of exoteric Christianity.

Lévi's books sold moderately well, but not well enough for him to live in even modest comfort, and he was forced to supplement his literary earnings by giving private lessons to those who wished to study the deeper aspects of 'occult science'. There were few of these personal pupils, but some of them were charged very high fees – Madame Blavatsky's aunt complained that she had to pay forty francs for one minute's conversation. No doubt Lévi regarded his rates as reasonable enough; he was extraordinarily complacent about both the value of the lessons he gave and the material rewards he received. He wrote:

> As regards our lessons – I have no manuscript course – I give to my disciples according to the need of their minds what the spirit gives me for them. I demand nothing, and I refuse nothing from them in return. It is a communion and an exchange of bread; spiritual for bodily. But the needs of the body are of so little account for me that the generous gifts of those of my children who are rich serve mainly to satisfy the first and greatest need of my soul and of all our souls: Charity.

Lévi's lessons were purely theoretical and his pupils were not introduced to any ritual working. This is not surprising – in fact Lévi himself had little experience of the practice of magic; almost the only ceremonial ever performed by him was that mentioned at the beginning of this chapter, the summoning of the shade of Apollonius of Tyana to visible appearance.

As this was a key experience for Lévi it is worth giving some extracts from Lévi's own account of it, for these illustrate both a Gothic romanticism and a curious ambivalence towards occult experiences – he never seems to have made up his mind whether they were objective, subjective, or some blend of the two.

Lévi's account is given in a straightforward enough way, but it is likely that his dramatic story of how he met the adept who made these workings possible is at least partly fictional:

> Returning one day to my hotel (he wrote) I found a note . . . containing half a transversely torn card, on which I recognized immediately the Seal of Solomon. With it was a small sheet of paper on which was written the message: 'Tomorrow at three o'clock, in front of Westminster Abbey, the other half of this card will be given to you.' I kept this curious appointment. A carriage was drawn up and as I held the card in my hand, an equerry approached, making a sign as he did so, and then opened the carriage door. It contained a veiled woman, dressed in black; she motioned me to sit beside her then showed me the other half of the card . . . 'Sir,' she began, 'I am aware that the law of secrecy is rigorous among Adepts; a friend of Sir B[ulwer] L[ytton], who has seen you, knows that you have been asked for phenomena and have refused to gratify such curiosity. You are possibly without the materials to do so; I would like to show you a complete magical cabinet, but I must exact beforehand an unbreakable promise of secrecy. If you cannot give me this promise I shall give orders for you to be driven to your hotel.' I made the required promise and I keep it faithfully by not disclosing the name, position or abode of this lady, whom I soon recognized as an initiate . . . We had numerous long conversations . . . she insisted upon the necessity of practical experience to complete initiation. She showed me a collection of magical robes and weapons, lent me some rare books and, in short, determined me to attempt at her house the experiment of a complete evocation, for which I prepared for a period of twenty-one days, scrupulously observing all the rules laid down . . .

Lévi gave these rules in the thirteenth chapter of his *Ritual*, and from them it appears that he must have spent the preparatory period eating vegetables, gazing at a portrait of Apollonius, and carrying on imaginary conversations with the long-dead sage. He could hardly have obeyed the injunction to study and meditate upon the writings of the deceased, for none of these have survived.

The ritual began with the kindling of two charcoal fires in copper chafing-dishes; on these were supposed to be burnt various 'perfumes' (i.e. varieties of incense), their purpose being to provide a dense smoke which would be used by the departed spirit in order to build up a material 'body'. Then Lévi began to read his ritual 'in a voice at first low but rising by degree'. After a while:

> The smoke spread, the flame first caused the objects upon which its light fell to waver and then expired, the smoke still floating about the altar; I seemed to feel a quaking of the earth, my ears tingled, my heart beat rapidly. I heaped more fuel and perfume upon the chafing-dishes, and as the flame again leapt up, I beheld distinctly before the altar, the figure of a man of more than normal size, which dissolved and vanished away. I recommenced the evocations . . . the mirror behind the altar seemed to brighten in its depth, in it became outlined a wan form, which uncreased and seemed to approach . . . Three times, with closed eyes, I invoked Apollonius. When I again looked there was a man in front of me, wrapped from head to foot in a shroud . . . He was lean, melancholy and beardless . . . I experienced an abnormally cold sensation, and when I endeavoured to question the phantom I could not utter a syllable. I therefore placed my hand on the Sign of the Pentagram, and pointed the sword at the figure, mentally commanding it to obey me . . . The form became vague and suddenly vanished. I ordered it to return and presently felt, as it were, a breath close by me; something touched my hand which was holding the sword, and immediately my fore-arm became numb. I guessed that the sword displeased the spirit, and I therefore placed its point downward, close by me, within the circle. At once

> the figure reappeared; but I experienced such a weakness in all my limbs, and a fainting sensation came so quickly over me, that I sat down, whereupon I fell into a profound lethargy accompanied by dreams of which I had only a confused recollection when I recovered consciousness. For several days afterwards my arm remained numb and painful.

The ghost did not speak to Lévi, but the two questions which he had intended to ask it, one on his own behalf, one on behalf of the woman adept, seemed to be answered in his own mind by an internal voice. Both answers were gloomy; the lady's reply – she had asked for information about a certain man – was 'Death', and Lévi's was similar.

Twice more Apollonius was evoked, each time with success, and on these occasions Lévi asked questions concerning the secrets of the qabalah. As, however, he recorded neither the contents of his questions nor the answers he received to them, we are unable to judge the truth of his claim that the departed philosopher revealed to him secrets 'which might change, in a short time, the foundations and laws of society at large, if they came to be generally known'. In spite of this bombastic statement the magician was sceptical about the exact nature of the experience which he had thrice undergone, affirming that he was not so hallucinated as to claim that he had really evoked, seen, and touched the great Apollonius, and warning others of the danger of repeating the experiment. He wrote:

> The effect of the preparations, the perfumes, the mirrors, the pantacles, is an actual drunkenness of the imagination, which must act powerfully upon a person of a nervous or impressionable nature. I do not explain the physical laws by which I saw and touched; I affirm only that I did see and did touch, apart from dreaming, and that this is enough to establish the real efficacy of magical ceremonies. For the rest, I regard the practice as destructive and dangerous . . . I commend the

greatest caution to those who propose devoting themselves to similar experiences; their result is intense exhaustion, and frequently a shock sufficient to occasion illness.

Lévi died in 1875, officially reconciled with the church of his birth, but very probably still retaining his own magical interpretation of the Christian creeds; six months later he was reincarnated as Aleister Crowley, or so, at any rate, the latter came to believe.

5 *Drugs, Demons and Duels*

Ten years after his death, Lévi was almost forgotten in his own country. The few disciples he had acquired during his life had dispersed; some had lost interest in occultism and others had died; still others, like Marie Gebhardt, had transferred their allegiance to the eastern occultism of Madame Blavatsky and the Theosophical Society. A few, however, still admired the writings of Lévi, among them Catulle Mendès. Mendès, the son-in-law of Gautier, was a novelist – his novels usually dealt with incest and other sexual peculiarities – and the editor of more than one literary journal. He had a wide literary acquaintance and one of his many friends was Stanislas de Guaita, a young aristocrat who was also a poet. In 1885 Catulle Mendès urged de Guaita, already the author of three books of verse, to read Lévi.

De Guaita took his friend's advice – and his life was transformed. He described his reading of Lévi's books as *le coup de foudre occultiste* – the occult clap of thunder, the happening which revealed to him his real destiny.

He abandoned his desire for literary fame; instead of frequenting the artistic salons of Paris he retired to his scarlet-draped study where, clad in a Cardinal's robe, he devoted his time to the study and practice of magic and alchemy. Sleeping during the day, if at all, working at night, using morphine, cocaine, and hashish to enable himself 'to project his astral body', he burned with an unquenchable desire to become a master-magician.

It was not long before he became acquainted with other

inhabitants of the cultural underworld of Parisian occultism. Two of these who particularly impressed him were, like himself, devoted to the memory of Eliphas Lévi; they were Gerard Encausse and Joseph Aimé Péladan.

Encausse was to become a practising physician, an expert hypnotist, and a writer on occultism under the pseudonym of Papus. Today he is chiefly remembered for his *Tarot of the Bohemians* (a book which, although valueless, still enjoys a certain reputation amongst occultists) and for his brief tenure of the position of unofficial charlatan-in-chief to the court of the last Czar of Russia – a position from which he was displaced by Rasputin. At the time he met de Guaita, however, he kept his magical proclivities to himself and was generally regarded as a bright young student who would very probably reach the top of his profession in course of time.

There have always been many peculiar people in the world of occultism, but it is likely that few have ever been quite so odd as Péladan. He seems to have inherited his eccentricity from his father (an enthusiastic advocate of homoeopathy who has been described by James Laver as being in a permanent state of cerebral intoxication) and he managed to combine extreme Catholicism with a profound admiration for the writings of Lévi and a belief in magic and reincarnation. Péladan affirmed that he was a reincarnation of an ancient Assyrian king and abandoned his christian names in favour of the Assyrian appellation of Sar Merodach (i.e., King Marduk). When he met de Guaita he was starving, living on a daily plate of boiled vegetables, although only a year or two previously he had published quite a successful novel – where the money it earned had gone remains a mystery. It was perhaps he who, in 1888, persuaded de Guaita to found a magical fraternity called the *Kabbalistic Order of the Rose-Croix*.

The authoritarian structure of this Order was made clear in the course of an article in the January 1889 issue of the French occult magazine *Initiation*:

> The organization shows us at its head a Council of twelve members, six of whom are known and of whom

six others remain unknown, ready to restore the Order if any circumstances whatsoever happen to destroy it. Besides one degree, exclusively practical, there are two others in it, subsidiary and theoretical, in which initiation is given. Every member takes an oath of obedience to the members of the Council, but his liberty is absolutely safeguarded, in that he may leave the society when it pleases him, under the sole condition of keeping secret the Order or the teaching received.

The six unknown members of the Council remain suitably unknown, but the other six were Péladan, Encausse (Papus), Paul Adam, a novelist, Ch. Barlet, Edouard Dupus, an addict to morphine who was to die in the course of giving himself an injection in a public urinal, and de Guaita himself. Magical orders never have a peaceful life under a collective leadership unless that leadership is made up on one strong character and several nonentities. The *Kabbalistic Order of the Rose-Croix* was no exception; the erotic Catholicism-cum-magic of Péladan and the more orthodox occultism of de Guaita were incompatible, and in 1890 the two magi parted company. Péladan then founded his own group, the *Order of the Rose-Croix of the Temple and the Grail or the Catholic Rose-Croix*, with a membership-list as brief as its title was long, while his place on the Council of Twelve was taken by a priest named Alta, a modernistically-inclined teacher at the Sorbonne.

The schism was accompanied by much acrimony, unpleasantness, bickering, and a certain amount of unfavourable newspaper coverage; but the latter was nothing to the storm of publicity that was to burst three years later and was to involve accusations of Black Magic, an alleged astral murder and two duels, one fought with pistols, the other with rapiers. All these events were the result of a peculiar quarrel between de Guaita and his fellow-occultists on the one hand and some of the later disciples of a half-mad prophet named Vintras on the other.

Vintras, to whose curious teachings Eliphas Lévi had at one time been inclined, was born in 1807, the illegitimate son of a servant girl. After a charity education he drifted from one unsatisfactory job to another before finding a temporary security as a works manager of a tiny cardboard-box factory; curiously enough several English sources describe his occupation in this factory as 'fireman', although they do not explain why a small business should have had such a full-time employee. The confusion seems to have arisen from a printer's error of over eighty years ago when a careless compositor transformed 'foreman' into 'fireman'.

One evening in August 1839, Vintras was writing in his office. Suddenly there came a knock on the door which then opened and admitted, not the expected workman, but an old man dressed in rags who addressed Vintras by his christian name and added: 'I am utterly tired, and wherever I go they treat me with disdain or as a thief.' The rest of the story is best told in Vintras' own words.

> I arose and placed a coin in his hand and made him understand that I wished him to leave. He . . . turned his back with a pained air . . . I shut the door after him and locked it. I did not hear him go down the stairs, so I called a workman . . . wishing him to search with me all the possible places which might conceal my old man, whom I had not seen go out. . . . I hunted through all the nooks and corners but found nothing. . . . I heard the bell ringing for mass . . . and ran back to my room to obtain a missal and, on the table where I had been writing, I found a letter . . . containing a refutation of heresy together with a profession of Catholic orthodoxy. . . . On the letter was lain the coin which I had given the old man.

All this seems ordinary enough, but Vintras decided that his visitor was the Archangel Michael, that he himself was the reincarnation of the prophet Elijah, and that his task was to inaugurate the coming 'Age of the Holy Ghost'. He abandoned his job, travelled round the country preaching his doctrines (he believed in the pre-existence of souls and that all, even Satan, would ultimately be redeemed) and soon built up a considerable following. He was a powerful preacher – he could never remember afterwards what he had said so one presumes he spoke while in a state of trance – and his disciples included not only unlettered men like himself but priests and aristocrats. He founded the Church of Carmel and, clad in vestments decorated with an inverted Cross (these being designed to indicate that 'the reign of the suffering Christ was over and the reign of the Holy Ghost had begun'), celebrated the *Provictimal Sacrifice of Mary*, a mass of his own devising, in his holy of holies. During these masses his followers, who appear to have been totally hysterical, saw empty chalices suddenly brim over with blood, smelt wondrous perfumes, beheld the consecrated host bleeding and even witnessed the Holy Ghost, in the form of a dove, perch on Vintras' shoulder. It was not surprising that the Roman Church quickly condemned the prophet for heresy or that, in 1842, after an unfair trial, he was sentenced to seven years' imprisonment on a charge of fraud.

After his release in 1848 he spent some years in London, an exile that was made more unpleasant than would otherwise have been the case by the activities of an ex-disciple, a priest named Gozzoli, who published in 1851 a pamphlet in which he accused the prophet of being homosexual, conducting secret masses at which both priests and people were naked, indulging in group sexual activities and masturbating at the foot of the altar. Gozzoli was an unpleasant character and was inclined to charge other people with vices to which he himself was inclined, but it is likely that there was at least a sub-stratum of truth in the accusations; unorthodox mysticism frequently goes hand-in-hand with unorthodox sex and there is no doubt that some of the later disciples of Vintras were sexual deviants.

Eventually Vintras returned to his native land where he died in 1875. Shortly before his death he made the acquaintance of an unfrocked priest named Boullan who had previously been imprisoned in France for fraud and in Rome for heresy. Boullan, born in 1824, had been a pious youth and, after his ordination to the priesthood, had become the confessor of a nun named Adèle Chevalier whom he eventually made his mistress. In 1859 the two founded the Society for the Reparation of Souls which specialised in unusual methods of exorcism – Boullan 'cured' 'demon-possessed' nuns by feeding them a mixture of consecrated communion wafers and human excrement – and, it seems, in Black Magic; for there is some evidence to show that on 8 January 1860 Boullan conducted a Black Mass at which he ritually sacrificed his own bastard child, born to Adèle Chevalier. After meeting Vintras he declared himself a convert to the teachings of the Church of Carmel and, when Vintras had died, he proclaimed himself as a reincarnation of John the Baptist and the new Supreme Pontiff.

Most of the members of the Church refused to accept Boullan's claim to leadership, but a few did so and settled with their chief in Lyons, a city which had retained a reputation for unorthodoxy since the Middle Ages. Whatever the truth may have been concerning the sexual teachings of Vintras himself it is unquestionable that Boullan taught a form of sexual magic. He held that the Fall of Man had been caused by an act of love on the part of Adam and Eve and that 'it was through acts of love accomplished in a religious spirit that the Redemption of Humanity could be achieved'. The evolutionary ladder, claimed Boullan, could be climbed more speedily by humanity if it partook of sexual intercourse with celestial beings; similarly, mankind could do the good deed of speeding up the evolution of brute creation by copulating with animals. In other words Boullan urged sexual relations with both incubi and succubi, the unclean demons of medieval theology, and with animals. He also taught his female disciples a method of having sex with his own astral body. There is no hard evidence that Boullan and his followers indulged in bestiality, although it is quite likely that they did so, but documents survive which prove that they engaged, or rather thought that they engaged, in sexual relations with angels, archangels, and the spirits of such historical figures as Cleopatra and Alexander the Great.

Stanislas de Guaita suspected the existence of these unorthodox activities and, late in 1886 he spent a fortnight in Lyons posing as a would-be convert to the Church of Carmel. Boullan was completely deceived; he welcomed the supposed convert with enthusiasm and initiated him into some of the inner mysteries of the Church. A month after de Guaita's return to Paris he was joined by a young man named Oswald Wirth, a former member of Carmel, who gave further details of Boullan's iniquities. The two decided that Boullan was, as they were later to write in their book *The Temple of Satan*, 'a pontiff of infamy, a base idol of the mystical Sodom, a magician of the worst type, a wretched criminal, an evil sorcerer, and the founder of an infamous sect'; accordingly they made a declaration of magical warfare upon Boullan, sending him a letter in which they affirmed that he was a condemned man.

'The pontiff of Carmel' was not the sort of man to capitulate to threats of this sort, so, deciding that the two Parisian magicians would attempt to put a spell upon him, he looked to his occult defences and put his establishment on a war footing. Soon the battle of the magicians was in full swing, with spells and curses being exchanged between Lyons and Paris and great spiritual struggles taking place on the astral plane – or so Boullan believed; de Guaita and Wirth on the other hand, claimed that these spells and astral struggles existed only in the Pontiff's imagination and that their letter of condemnation referred only to their forthcoming literary exposure of Carmel and its chief.

This occult struggle, real or imaginary, was to last for almost five years and to end only with Boullan's death. Two years after its commencement the novelist J.K. Huysmans, at one time a disciple of Zola but already undergoing the inner psychological changes that were ultimately to reconcile him with the Catholic Church, was drawn into the battle by his desire to learn something about Satanism, about which he was planning to write a novel. Huysmans already knew of Boullan's reputation and, thinking it likely that the latter was either a Satanist or could put him

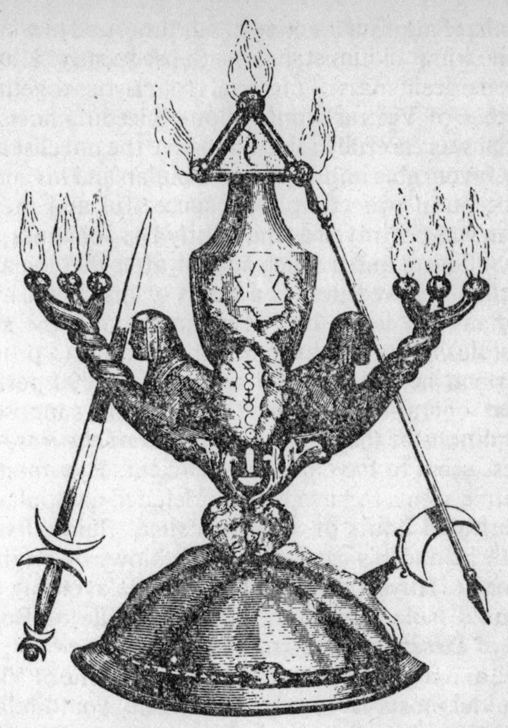

A number of magical implements – lamp, wand, sword and dagger – drawn by Lévi and which appeared in his *Transcendental Magic*, 1896 edition.

in touch with Satanists, wrote to him asking him for reliable information on the subject of devil-worship and offering to depict him in his forthcoming novel as 'the Superman, the Satanist, the only one in existence, far removed from the spiritism of the occultists'. It is surprising that Boullan was not offended by this offer, for he affected a mask of piety hardly compatible with being publicised as a super-Satanist. Nevertheless he replied in a friendly manner, assuring Huysmans that he was 'an Adept who had declared war on all demoniacal cults' and offering to loan 'documents which will enable you to prove that Satanism is active in our time, and in what form and in what circumstances'. Subsequently Huysmans received a great mass of material from Lyons together with a number of Vintras's miraculous 'bleeding hosts'. This material was carefully selected to give the novelist an altogether favourable impression of Boullan and his activities; the deception was completely successful and in *Là-Bas* Boullan was portrayed as the saintly Dr. Johannes, enemy of all Satanism and a much sought-after theologian.

Boullan believed that as a result of his friendship with Huysmans the latter had been drawn into the struggle against de Guaita and his minions. Anxious to protect his new friend he twice in the summer of 1890 performed magical operations designed to foil the supposed evil machinations of the *Kabbalistic Order of the Rose-Croix*.

These seem to have been insufficient. Huysmans, who for a time seems to have been as deluded as Boullan himself, suffered bouts of what he called 'fluidic fisticuffs' – both he and his cat were struck blows by an invisible antagonist. Huysmans took appropriate avoiding action. He would isolate himself, burn a pastille of Boullan's 'paste of exorcism', a mixture of camphor, cloves, frankincense and myrrh, and then, brandishing one of Vintras's miraculous hosts in his right hand, he would 'clasp the blessed scapular of Carmel close to his body and recite conjurations which dissolved the astral fluids and paralysed the power of the sorcerers'.

Huysmans took these events with the utmost seriousness; during the summer of 1891 he spent several weeks in Lyons where elaborate ceremonies were performed for his protection. He reported to a friend: 'The battles have begun again since I last wrote to you. . . . Boullan jumps about like a tiger-cat holding one of his hosts. He invokes the aid of St. Michael and the eternal justiciaries . . . standing at his altar he cries out "Strike down Péladan, strike down Péladan." '

It was not Péladan who was struck down, however, but Boullan himself. He suddenly collapsed and died on 3 January 1893, the day before he was due to go to Paris to lecture upon the qabalah. In spite of the fact that Boullan suffered from heart trouble and a morbid liver condition Huysmans was shocked by his friend's sudden death, which he felt was probably the result of Black Magic – an opinion shared by Jules Bois, a former member of the Church of Carmel. The latter promptly published an article in *Gil-Blas* in which he specifically accused de Guaita and Péladan of 'astral murder'. The following day a journalist interviewed Huysmans and reported him as saying: 'It is indisputable that de Guaita and Péladan practise Black Magic every day. Poor Boullan was perpetually engaged in conflict with the evil spirits they continually sent him from Paris. . . . It is quite possible that my poor friend Boullan has succumbed to a supremely powerful spell.' That same evening Huysmans and his cat were subjected to a particularly severe infliction of 'fluidic fisticuffs'.

Worse was to follow: infuriated at being publicly branded as a diabolist and murderer de Guaita challenged both Jules Bois and Huysmans to duels and sent his seconds to call upon them. Huysmans found the prospect of physical conflict less pleasant than that of astral battle and apologised through his own seconds, stating that he was not responsible for the statements of Jules Bois and that he himself had not intended to 'impugn the honour of de Guaita'. At first it seemed that de Guaita's quarrel with Jules Bois would also be settled peacefully, but the latter repeated his allegations, this time also involving Dr Encausse (Papus) in his accusations of astral homicide. Two duels resulted.

The first of these, that between Jules Bois and de Guaita, was accompanied by a number of curious incidents. One of Jules Bois' seconds, Paul Foucher, gave an interesting account of these:

> . . . . Bois said to me, as we were leaving for Meudon, where the duel was to take place: "You will see something very singular happen. On both sides our allies are praying for us and practising conjurations." Something strange did indeed happen on the road to Versailles.

One of the horses in our carriage stopped suddenly and began to tremble, then it staggered as though it had seen the Devil in person. It was impossible to proceed. The trembling lasted for twenty minutes.

The duel nevertheless took place and, thanks be to God, or perhaps to the Devil, two bullets were exchanged without result. Such, at least was believed, but several days later, when I was engaging in practice shots at Gastine-Renette's, the famous gunsmith said to me: 'What happened the other day? The bullet of one of the duellists didn't leave the barrel. My employee noted it when he was cleaning the pistols.'

I was sure that the pistol of Jules Bois had not missed fire. As for the pistol used by Monsieur de Guaita, it is quite unbelievable that neither he nor his seconds, one of whom was an officer and the other was Laurent Tailhade, should not have noticed that the pistol did not fire. The occultists could therefore pride themselves on having terrified the horse of one of the opponents and having prevented the bullet from leaving the pistol of Monsieur de Guaita.

The second duel, fought three days later between Encausse and Jules Bois with rapiers, was also notable for its magical aspects, and, once again, horses were involved. The horse drawing Bois' carriage to the duelling field collapsed, he engaged a second carriage; again the horse collapsed, this time throwing Bois violently to the ground. Nevertheless, he kept his appointment (although he arrived bruised, cut and bleeding) and was suitably impressed by the appearance of his opponent. 'I remember,' he wrote, 'Papus taking off his coat. . . . I remember the swords, the gypsy eye of my adversary, the impatient wrinkle in his forehead, his beard and jovial lips, his heavy build. He was a bull among these improvised evangelists.'

Both duellists were wounded in the course of the encounter, but neither seriously, for, as Paul Foucher said, 'although the swords were magical, the wounds they inflicted were slight and have long been healed'. Shortly afterwards the two were reconciled and Jules Bois seems to have realised that, morally speaking, he had been on the wrong side.

Stanislas de Guaita died in 1897 from an overdose of drugs. He was succeeded as chief of the *Kabbalistic Order of the Rose-Croix* by Ch. Barlet who soon resigned from the position in favour of Papus. In 1899 Papus made an unsuccessful attempt at reunification with the Péladan group, following which he seems to have administered the Order in a way which repelled and antagonised a number of French occultists. Sédir, who had been expelled from the Order by Papus, sourly commented shortly before the 1914–18 war: 'For several years the foundation of the lamented Marquis de Guaita has risked seeing its original character changed; most of the scholars, who were its glory, have gradually disappeared, and some students, doubtless sincere but perhaps too eager for titles, parchments, and phenomena, have sought to take their places. . . .'

The annoyance of Sédir appears to have resulted from Papus' enthusiasm for physical alchemy – the attempt to turn base metals into gold and to discover the Elixir of Life – and his willingness to confer and receive high-sounding but meaningless occult dignities.

After the death of Papus in 1917 the Order split up into several schismatic and competing sects. Perhaps the most interesting of these was the small alchemical group centred at Douai and under the leadership of M. Jolivet-Castelot, a man who claimed to have successfully manufactured gold 'although in small quantity only'.

This gentleman was also the founder (1914) of the Alchemical Society of France. He held that the 22 major trumps of the Marseilles tarot, as rectified by Lévi and others, were a symbolic revelation of the theory and practice of alchemy. He publicised his beliefs, firstly, in a short article published in the occult journal *L'Initiation* (November 1896, Vol. 33 No. 2) and then, at much greater length, in his *How to Become an Alchemist – A*

Treatise on the Spagyric Art and Hermeticism Founded on the Keys of the Tarot.

Alchemy has been a continuing preoccupation with French occultists for over two hundred years but M. Jolivet-Castelot's theories and experiments were regarded with disapproval by a number of his fellow seekers for the Stone of the Philosophers. He was not, it was claimed, a real alchemist but merely an unorthodox chemist. Writing in the periodical *Le Voile d'Isis* in 1926, M. Auriger stated in his article *Alchemy and Science*:

> M. Jolivet-Castelot will, I am sure, allow me to make one remark about the use of the word 'alchemical' as applied to his experiments. It would have been correct in the days when only alchemists undertook this kind of work; but nowadays the materials and methods derive from the domain of chemistry pure and simple. If they were alchemical in the true sense of the word there would be . . . not a single Professor . . . however learned, capable of verifying them. Besides, since M. Jolivet-Castelot asks for verification only by chemists, it means that the transmutations he claims have been achieved by chemical means and in no other way.

The adepts who were so contemptuous of 'mere chemistry' were often men far odder than M. Jolivet-Castelot in both their lives and their opinions, mingling alchemy with strange sexual cults and even devil-worship. Take, for example, Jean-Julien Champagne, a painter and draughtsman of talent – a splendid drawing by him provided the frontispiece for *Le Mystère de Cathédrales*, supposedly written by the adept Fulcanelli – who also practised magic, studied alchemy and worshipped Lucifer.

Champagne (*circa* 1885-1932) spoke largely in *argot*, which he believed to have some esoteric significance, claiming that it was a 'spoken qabalah' and that its name had some etymological connection with *Art Gothique* (Gothic art) and *Art Goetique* (black magic). He drank large amounts of absinthe, even after its use was made illegal in 1914, and took alchemical pupils although his 'laboratory equipment' consisted of no more than an ordinary household stove and few flasks and retorts. He seems to have possessed a ripe sense of humour – a rare quality amongst dedicated occultists – and made his pupils sleep with great bags of charcoal and coke in their beds in order that they might 'come to a true understanding of the mystery of Fire'.

As John Symonds has remarked in another connection, an occultist without a magical order is like a politician without a party; Champagne was concerned in two esoteric brotherhoods, one of which, the Fraternity of Heliopolis, was founded by him. In spite of occult legends concerning the power and influence of the Heliopolitans they seem to have been few in number and their activities obscure and ineffectual. The other secret society in which Champagne involved himself was dedicated to the worship of Lucifer, the fallen Star of the Morning, identified by the author of the *Apocalypse* with Satan. According to Pierre Geyraud, author of two fascinating studies of Parisian occultism, both published in 1939, Champagne was one of the founders of this Luciferian sect. He wrote:

> Champagne helped to organise a Luciferian Society in the Saint-Merry district, with a strictly limited membership, and himself designed the Baphomet – an androgynous demon with the head and feet of a goat – for the inner sanctum, where ritual meetings were held. To this Templar figure, whose right arm hangs down while the left is raised in the traditional alchemical gesture of *solve et coagulo* [dissolve and solidify], he added a mitred arse under the right hand, while the left hand brandished an emblem impossible to describe. . . . In 1932, Champagne is said to have died a horrible, lingering death . . . for having betrayed the Society. After a long drawn struggle, his body tortured by fearful abscesses that seemed like some form of leprosy, he was buried in the cemetery of Villiers-le-Bel. A Latin inscription . . . tells us that here lies an apostle of hermetic science: *Apostolus Hermeticae Scientiae*.

In 1922 Champagne was present, along with a chemist named Gaston Sauvage, at an alchemical experiment which took place in the unlikely surroundings of the gasworks at Sarcelles. In this experiment Eugène Canseliet succeeded – if his own account is to be believed – in transmuting a hundred grams of base metal into purest gold. The 'Powder of Projection' used to achieve this remarkable result was not manufactured by M. Canseliet himself but was supplied to him as a gift by his hermetic Master, 'Fulcanelli'.

Who exactly was Fulcanelli? Seemingly an Adept who has discovered not only the secret of making gold but something very like the medicine of everlasting life. For those who have met him over the years, notably M. Canseliet and his associates, report that, far from ageing, he seems to be getting younger and younger – when Canseliet first met Fulcanelli the latter appeared to be about eighty years old, but thirty years later he seemed to be no more than fifty. It is to be hoped that from time to time this rejuvenation process reverses itself, or at least stops short, otherwise Fulcanelli's pupils will eventually be forced to wheel their beloved Master about in a perambulator.

It is not only in his capacity for reversing time that Fulcanelli has shown himself to be a superman. On at least one occasion he has revealed a knowledge of both advanced physics and of the future development of that science. For another man who claims to have met him – Jacques Bergier, the scientist-turned-writer who co-authored the best selling *Morning of the Magicians* – has reported that in June 1937 Fulcanelli told him that it was easy to split the atom, that artificially created radioactivity could poison the global atmosphere within a few years, and that with a small amount of metal whole cities could be destroyed. When Bergier seemed sceptical Fulcanelli became angry. 'You think,' he said, 'that alchemists do not understand the structure of the atom and therefore can never have succeeded in liberating nuclear energy nor transmuting metals . . . but . . . geometrical arrangements of extremely pure substances suffice to liberate atomic forces . . .'

Then Fulcanelli went on to read aloud an extract from a book by Nobel Prizewinner Frederick Soddy in which the pioneer expert on radium stated that he believed that in the far past there had existed forgotten civilisations which had destroyed themselves by the misuse of atomic energy. Fulcanelli concluded with a warning. 'I ask you to remember,' he said, 'that alchemists have always taken religious and moral issues into consideration in their researches, while modern physics were born . . . from the amusements of a few nobles and rich libertines. Science without conscience . . . I believe that I am doing my duty by warning a few research students . . . but I have no hope that my warnings will bear fruit . . . I have no reason to hope.'

Such statements, if really dating from 1937, are indeed remarkable, for they were made some years before a number of eminent physicists wrote to President Roosevelt stating that they believed it might be possible to make an atomic bomb. Even more astonishing was Fulcanelli's remark concerning the achievement of fission by the 'geometrical arrangements of extremely pure substances', for this sounds like an anticipation of atomic piles, those 'geometrical arrangements' of uranium rods and inert dampers that are to be found in every nuclear power plant.

But if these statements *were* made in 1937 – for however honest M. Bergier may have been his memory may have been blurred when he told of them more than eight years later – were they made by Fulcanelli? That is, were they made by the same man who supplied M. Canseliet with the 'Powder of Projection' in 1922? Did, in fact, Fulcanelli ever exist outside the imagination of those who claimed to be, or to have been, his pupils? Most non-occultists who have considered the question have answered No.

It is true, of course, that two books supposedly written by Fulcanelli were published some fifty years or so ago. But who was their real author? Some have suggested

M. Canseliet himself – certainly it was he who delivered Fulcanelli's manuscripts to the publisher, wrote fulsome introductions to them and, over the years collected the royalties on their sales. On the other hand it would seem that there are notable stylistic differences between the writings of M. Canseliet and those of his supposed teacher.

A more likely candidate would appear to be Jean-Julien Champagne, the absinthe-swilling worshipper of Lucifer and founder of the Fraternity of Heliopolis, of which brotherhood, states the introduction to *Le Mystère des Cathédrales*, 'Fulcanelli' was a member. It is significant that during the years when M. Canseliet was acting as a literary agent for the great alchemist he was living in the same house as M. Champagne, and that curious theories, e.g. that about *argot* (which M. Champagne is known to have held years before the publication of Fulcanelli's writings), were incorporated into those same writings. Even more remarkable is the fact that several close acquaintances of Jean-Julien Champagne have reported that he told them in confidence that he was the 'real Fulcanelli'.

A contemporary French alchemist, astrologer and admirer of Lévi is M. Armand Barbault, of whose existence there is no doubt at all.

M. Barbault became a student of alchemy before World War II and soon afterwards began practical experimentation designed to produce a miraculous medicine somewhat like the 'potable gold' of Paracelsus and other 16th century iatro-alchemists. As his 'first matter', the substance on which he worked, he used 'earth' – which may or may not mean ordinary garden loam – and for its maturation he applied to it a 'secret fire' compounded of dew and sap. He decided to use dew because the fourth plate of the *Mutus Liber*, an alchemical classic, shows a number of cloths stretched out on poles, perhaps to catch dew, and another cloth being wrung out into a dish by a man and a woman. The same plate shows the stretched out cloths being regarded by a bull and a ram, perhaps signifying the zodiacal signs of Taurus and Aries, and both sun and moon visible in the heavens. This and other factors led M. Barbault to attach great importance to carrying out his operations in accordance with correct astrological conditions. It is to be presumed that these were comparatively rare, for the maturation of his earth took him no less than 22 years. Twenty-two is also the number of the letters in the Hebrew alphabet and the major trumps of the Marseilles tarot deck – facts which Lévi's present-day followers see as being of great numerological importance.

Finally, early in the 1960s, the amazing elixir was perfected and sent to a pharmaceutical laboratory for analysis and evaluation. Somehow one is not surprised to learn that it not only proved impossible to analyse but that 'nothing even vaguely resembling it could be discovered'. According to Raymond Abellio, who contributed a preface to Barbault's *Gold of a Thousand Mornings*, the pharmacists who vainly attempted to discover the exact composition of the tincture began to speak of a 'new category of matter endowed with mysterious, possibly vital, properties'.

M. Barbault was not satisfied with this achievement, but went on towards the preparation of the Philosopher's Stone by striving to bring his preparation to 'the second degree of perfection' in spite of meteorological and astrological annoyances. He complained that 'the sap is not sufficiently plentiful or rich because two eclipses in Aries and the conjunction of Saturn with the new moon coincided with a frost that damaged plants. . . .' All was not lost, however, for M. Barbault added that a 'Stone' he had prepared promised well, for it was covered with small crystals and within its mass were numbers of starry specks; this meant, decided the alchemist, that 'Philosophical Mercury' was ready to 'emerge from its matrix'.

As well as alchemists and magicians whose ideology is, in the last analysis, derived from the writings of Eliphas Lévi and his school it is likely that there are still some present-day disciples of the occult 'Catholicism' of Vintras. Certainly such still survived in Paris shortly before World War II, for Pierre Geyraud, whose description of Jean-Julien Champagne has already been quoted, reported his own attendance at one of their rites.

Geyraud, whose personal attitude towards magic was ambivalent, was suspicious that a group of devil-worshippers who had been annoyed by his investigations were casting evil spells on him. He sought help from white magicians of his acquaintance and, on the advice of one of them, had a Vintrasian priest and priestess say the 'Mass of the Sacrifice of Glory of Melchizedek' for his spiritual and physical well-being.

The rite was celebrated in the bedroom of an unassuming apartment in the Javel district. The 'altar' was a chest of drawers with its frontal scarlet cloth. Liturgically, this is the colour of fire and blood and is used in the church to symbolise both the fire of the spirit which descended at Pentecost and the blood shed on Calvary and by the martyrs. Presumably the Vintrasians were using it at their Mass as a reminder that Melchizedek, that strange Old Testament king who bore bread and wine to Abraham, was an antetype of Christ.

On the improvised altar were placed two 'chalices' – champagne glasses – a plate of communion wafers, and a lighted candle. The priestess wore white robes and a green cape and the priest – her husband – scarlet vestments with an inverted white cross, the arms of which lay across his genitals to 'symbolise the crucifixion of the phallus'.

After an invocation of the Archangel Michael, presumably identified with Vintras himself, white wine was poured into one glass, red into another. After the consecration of the elements the priest muttered incomprehensible prayers, presumably formulae of exorcism, singed two wafers in the candle flame, and offered one of them to Geyraud with the statement, 'Here is the communion of bread and fire.' Geyraud refused the offer which, he said, seemed to annoy the priest – perhaps not surprising if, as would seem to be the case, the latter was, out of pure goodness of heart, conducting a complex ceremony in order to protect Geyraud from satanic manifestations.

Priest and priestess communicated in both kinds, he drinking the red wine, she the white, and the Mass concluded with an invocation of the Holy Spirit.

It is unlikely that there have ever been any British or American Vintrasians – though there have been believers in the essentially similar Mariavite heresy in both the USA and the UK – but for the last 120 years or so there have been English-speaking alchemists and magicians who have followed the teachings of Eliphas Lévi and his school.

6 *Lévi's English Disciples*

In the heyday of High Victorianism – the 'fifties and 'sixties of the last century – a minority of the unmarried young men and women of the English middle clasess found the moral stuffiness and stiff conventionality of their social milieu well-nigh insupportable.

The women amongst these rebels tended to react against the tedium of the unvarying daily round by either taking refuge in emotional religiosity – usually evangelical or Tractarian – or by sinking unhappily into that sort of semi-voluntary invalidism typified by Elizabeth Barrett.

The men had a wider choice available to them. Alternatives to Exeter Hall and Puseyite vicarages were provided by the proprietors of such resorts as the Coal Hole and the Cider Cellars. Here, forgetful of cucumber sandwiches and Gunpowder tea, sweet madeira and seedcake, the sons of merchants and manufacturers could enjoy a classless bonhomie. The rank cigars could be smoked, the overpriced sparkling Moselle could be swilled, and the choruses of such songs as 'He'll no more grind a girl' could be bellowed again and again. Afterwards, those willing to run the risk of the pox and the remedies against it[1], could purchase their pleasures from the painted whores who thronged the Haymarket and Leicester Square.

Some who rebelled against the complacencies of the Victorian environment were more concerned with spirit and mind than they were with the flesh. Such as these felt that the prevailing Anglo-Saxon literary and artistic orthodoxies were as stifling to the soul as the dominant moral standards were repressive to the body. For them the totality of French culture – not only its writing and its painting but its temporary fads and fashions – were all important. To read a French poet rather than an English one, to go to a Parisian rather than a London theatre, even to choose to drink *vin ordinaire* rather than bitter beer – each was felt, in some indefinable way, to be a shout of defiance against the inanities of the English bourgeoisie. A few, a very few, of these intellectual rebels discovered magic, raised the oriflamme of Hermes against the manifestoes of the Manchester School, and became the first English-speaking disiples of Eliphas Lévi.

Even before this, however, there had been a minor English revival of magical study and experiment. More than one of the professional astrologers who flourished in the period 1780–1850 had dabbled in talismanic magic, manufacturing and consecrating charms designed to attract money and love, ward off unfavourable planetary influences, and baffle the hostility of enemies. This revival had its literary side; periodicals such as the strangely named *Straggling Astrologer* made something of a feature of articles devoted to ritual magic.

More significant – for it still has its admirers today – was the publication of Francis Barrett's *The Magus* in 1801. This curious compilation presented the techniques taught by the grimoires and such renaissance writers as Cornelius Agrippa in an ossified, codified, but easily comprehended form. Almost nothing is known of Barrett himself but there is some reason to believe that he founded a school of magic and many years ago the late Montague Summers, an irregularly but possibly validly ordained priest, reported that he had been told that

> . . . Francis Barrett actually founded a small sodality of students of these dark and deep mysteries, and . . . under his tuition – for he was profoundly learned in these things – some advanced far upon the path of transcendental wisdom. One at least was a Cambridge man, of what status – whether an undergraduate or

the Fellow of a College – I do not know, but there is reason to believe that he initiated others, and until quite recent years – it perhaps persists even today – the Barrett tradition was maintained at Cambridge, but very privately, and his teaching has been handed on to promising subjects.

Apart from this one of us, many years ago, was given a brief sight of diaries and papers purporting to be those of a pupil of Barrett.

Amongst the Victorians who experimented with practical occultism, particularly crystal-gazing, was a tea merchant named Frederick Hockley, a bibliophile with a collection of grimoires and similar works, both manuscript and printed, who was, according to an occult legend, a pupil of a man who had been initiated by Barrett. Hockley was friendly with a number of young would-be magicians, and numbered amongst them was Kenneth Mackenzie – probably the first of the English-speaking intellectual rebels referred to earlier, who turned to the writings of Eliphas Lévi in their quest for enlightenment.

As a youth Mackenzie had been a sceptic, a rationalist admirer of the writings of Jeremy Bentham and his fellow-utilitarians. He had experienced, however, a remarkable supernatural manifestation which had convinced him of human survival after bodily death and first aroused his interest in occult phenomena.

The experience in question had its origin in a conversation between Mackenzie and his friend Theodore Buckley, an Oxford clergyman. At the close of the discussion the two men entered into a pact that whichever of them died first would endeavour to appear, in spirit form, to the other 'to indicate the certainty and reality of life beyond the grave'.

In 1856, on the Festival of King Charles the Martyr, Buckley died at the age of thirty. Three days later, at about 12.30 a.m., Mackenzie was lying in bed, quite unaware of the death of his friend. Suddenly he felt as though a cold, clammy hand had very gently been placed upon his forehead. He turned round to see what had caused this peculiar sensation and saw 'the spirit of Buckley in his usual dress, standing at his bedside with a portfolio under his arm exactly as he had so often seen him in life'. Mackenzie stated that as soon as he had recognised the apparition as being that of his old friend it retreated towards the window but after 'remaining there most distinctly visible both in form and feature for more than two minutes, it slowly faded away'.

The sight of this apparition, which he claimed to have again seen on two subsequent occasions, changed the course of Mackenzie's life. He began to attend séances and to study the physical phenomena of spiritualism, already very much in the news since the commencement, in the previous year, of the spectacular mediumistic career of D.D. Home. At about the same time he read Lévi's *Dogme de la Haute Magie* and fell completely under the influence of the French magician's limpid style and distorted but ingenious versions of occult tradition. By 1861, when the Englishman visited Paris and had two long interviews with his hero, Mackenzie regarded Lévi with an admiration that approached veneration. It is probable that Lévi was amused by the solemnity of his visitor – who actually mistook his host's tobacco jar for an ancient and valuable statuette of the Egyptian goddess Isis – for he indulged in a good deal of leg-pulling, telling him of unlikely dreams he claimed to have had and informing him that the *Zohar* (a mediaeval qabalistic book of about the same length as the Old Testament) was of such a size that it took several loaded ox-waggons to move about even one copy of the work.

Nevertheless, Mackenzie remained fascinated by magic, which he defined as 'a psychological branch of science, dealing with the sympathetic effects of stones, drugs, herbs, and living substances upon the imaginative and reflective faculties', and became an advanced occultist, claiming that he had been initiated into the legendary *Rosicrucian Fraternity* and studying the 'Enochian magical system' of the 16th century occultists John Dee and Edward Kelley. He spent a good deal of time in Europe – both his German and French were excellent – and it is at least possible that working-notes made by him of rituals he had witnessed in some continental magical temple supplemented by extracts from the writings of Levi and bits of Enochian magic were the basis of the occult cipher manuscripts that were discovered by a Notting Hill clergyman among the papers of Mackenzie's old friend Hockley who had died in 1885. It was the discovery and decipherment of these papers that led to the foundation of the Golden Dawn.

For a year or so after he had found the manuscripts the Notting Hill clergyman did nothing about them, but in the summer of 1887 he passed them to his friend Dr. W. Wynn Westcott, asking him if they could be decoded and, if so, whether it was his opinion that the job was worth doing. Westcott, who recognized the code as one traditionally used by alchemists, replied that he thought the manuscripts might be of great magical importance and that he would get a friend who had for some time been enjoying his hospitality, a certain S.L. MacGregor Mathers, to perform the irksome task of decipherment.

Westcott and Mathers shared an interest in occultism but had very little else in common. The former habitually wore a frock-coat and wanted above all else to be considered respectable; the latter cared little about his personal appearance, although sometimes he wore full Highland dress – in which, so he said, he 'felt like a flame walking' – rode a bicycle, affected Jacobite principles and had a burning desire to be a Master of Magic. It is perhaps not surprising that two such incompatible characters ultimately fell out with one another.

Westcott had been born in 1848, had studied both law and medicine, becoming an expert in medical jurisprudence, and had eventually been appointed Queen's Coroner for North-east London. As the area in which his inquests were conducted included Hoxton, then a poverty-stricken slum with many gin-palaces and a sizeable criminal population, he soon became a recognised authority on alcoholism, murder, suicide, and every form of sudden death. He was interested in almost every variety of occultism, although he tried to keep his medical colleagues unaware of these unorthodox leanings, was a friend of the Russian occultist Madame Blavatsky, an advocate of the mystical Christianity of Anna Kingsford (a woman whose visions seem to have owed more to ether and chloroform addiction than to genuine religious experience), and an enthusiastic reader of alchemical tracts, qabalistic treatises, and the writings of Eliphas Lévi. Westcott was also a dedicated freemason and it is probable that he first met S.L. MacGregor Mathers at either some masonic function or at a meeting of Madame Blavatsky's Theosophical Society; both men had enjoyed an intellectual flirtation with the pseudo-oriental occultism of that organisation.

MacGregor Mathers had been born in 1854 as plain George Samuel Liddel Mathers, the son of Willam Mathers, a London commercial clerk. The latter must have enjoyed a reasonably good income for he educated his son at the reputable, if at the time slightly obscure, Bedford Grammar School. Nevertheless, when he died he left his widow in what were coyly referred to as 'reduced circumstances' and she and her son retired to Bournemouth where they lived quietly upon her small income – presumably an annuity or pension of some sort, for it ceased entirely at her death and her son inherited nothing. Even before his mother's death the younger Mathers had begun to style himself 'G.S.L. MacGregor Mathers, Comte de Glenstrae'; he claimed that the name Mather was an anglicised form of the Gaelic *Mo Athair*, the posthumous one, a name adopted by some of the MacGregors after the proscription of their clan, and that he was fully entitled to revive the title of Comte de Glenstrae which had, so he said, been conferred upon his great-grandfather by a Bourbon king in recognition of his services to the French cause in India. He failed, however, to explain why a French monarch shoud have conferred a title pertaining to an obscure Scottish valley. Almost certainly the title was imaginary, a fantasy born of

Lévi's drawing of the Sabbatic Goat, which he regarded as a rectified version of the tarot trump known as *The Devil*.

Mathers' Jacobite sympathies and Celtic revivalism. According to one report, from an admittedly hostile source, he only visited Scotland on one occasion, suffering from a heavy cold throughout his visit, finding the climate unpleasant and the food uneatable.

At no time in his life did Mathers ever find paid employment, but he was always extremely busy and while living in Bournemouth his main preoccupations were masonic and military. He was a member of the Volunteers – the ancestor of today's Territorial Army – and was an enthusiastic amateur swordsman, although it may be that he had more energy than skill, for he acquired the livid scar of a sabre cut upon his right cheek and bore this token of his martial proclivities for the rest of his life. He had been made a mason in the Hengist Lodge at Christchurch, Hampshire, and was also an initiate of various chivalric and high-grade masonic fraternities. His interest in these, in occultism in general, and magic in particular, had been first aroused by his reading of *Zanoni*, a three-volume occult novel written by that same Bulwer Lytton whose female friend had supplied Lévi with the magical apparatus used by him in his evocation of the shade of Apollonius. Mathers told Brodie-Innes, a friend of his later years, that he almost fell in love with the character of the magician-hero Zanoni. Certainly he so much identified himself with Lytton's creation that he was nicknamed 'Zan' by his intimates and after his marriage his wife called him by that name until the day of his death. Hoping to discover the forgotten secrets that would enable him to transform himself into another Zanoni, a semi-divine magician holding the keys of life, death, and initiation, Mathers threw himself into the study of the dusty literature of qabalism, alchemy, and magic with the same enthusiasm that he had previously devoted to musketry and marching drill. He began to translate into English some of the books of the *Zohar*, that jumbled storehouse of Jewish mysticism and magic, not from the Aramaic Chaldee in which someone, probably a Spanish Jew named Moses de Leon, had originally written them, but from the 17th century Latin version of the German scholar, Knorr von Rosenroth.

Mathers had probably completed his translation, later to be published under the title of *The Kabbalah Unveiled*, by the time he left Bournemouth for London. In any case he had done so when he met Madame Blavatsky, in 1886, for he lent her a copy of his unpublished manuscript and she quoted from it in her *Secret Doctrine*, the book that became the Bible of devout Theosophists.

When Mathers had completed his decoding of the mysterious manuscripts, a task he must have found tedious rather than difficult, for the alphabetic code in which they were written was simple enough, he found their contents of peculiar interest. They included both a description of five hitherto unknown and magically orientated initiation rituals and a good deal of rather abstruse occult teaching – for example a new and, to Mathers, revolutionary method of attributing the twenty-two trumps of the tarot cards to the letters of the Hebrew alphabet.

With the manuscript, so Westcott asserted, was an intimation that further information might be obtained from a German Rosicrucian adept named Fraulein Sprengel. Westcott, so he said, wrote to her at an address in Nuremberg, thus beginning a protracted correspondence. Much advanced teaching was given and – it was claimed – the German magician signed a charter authorising the establishment of an English 'Temple' conferring, by means of ceremonial initiations, the five occult grades described in the cipher manuscript.

Magic is essentially a hierarchic philosophy and the idea of an evolutionary ladder of 'grades' or 'degrees' is an integral part of it. The idea seems to have originated in classical times when the universe was pictured as a series of concentric spheres with God, Aristotle's prime mover, as the outermost, then the sphere of the fixed stars, then the seven spheres of the planets known to antiquity, then, finally, the sphere of the earth, the sub-lunar world of change and decay. The conception was taken over by the gnostics – those cultists, some pagan, some nominally Christian, who saw neither faith, nor works, but knowledge as the key to salvation – who believed that the human soul must travel up through the spheres, back to God, in order to obtain redemption. It was generally supposed that this rising through the spheres was a post-mortem experience, but some cults held that it could be achieved while still in the body and that the initiate who had achieved or partially achieved this would be possessed of supernatural powers; he who had successfully reached, say, the sphere of Jupiter would have the magical powers of that sphere and of all the spheres below it.

A similar system of spiritual gradation can be discerned in some qabalistic treatises. For although in its highest aspects the qabalah expresses a pure and exalted mysticism, an attempt to resolve into a higher unity the contradiction between the conceptions of immanent and transcendent Deity, there is no doubt that underlying it is a substratum of magic and superstition, that some qabalists have held to an essentially magical and semi-polytheistic interpretation of the universe, and that these latter have believed in a progression through successive spheres very similar to that previously described. It was these magical aspects of qabalism that had most appealed to Mathers and other western occultists who had studied the system, and the magical grades devised by them supposedly equated with various stages of the progression up the rungs of the spiritual ladder.

Of the five grades described in the cipher manuscripts the first two related to the sphere of earth and in them the magician was supposed to obtain perfect control over his physical body and its material surroundings; the third grade corresponded to the sphere of the Moon and the fourth and fifth grades to the spheres of Mercury and Venus.

On the basis of the claimed continental authorisation Mathers and Westcott set up their London Temple – officially called 'the Isis-Urania Temple of the Hermetic Golden Dawn' – in March 1888. At first the membership of the Order was very small but it soon began to grow, for its dramatic rituals, glamorous atmosphere of secrecy and western terminology appealed to those who were drawn towards occultism but repelled by the bad Sanskrit and general oriental bias of the Theosophical Society and its leadership. For the first three years of its existence the Golden Dawn taught only the theory of magic and not its practice. Its initiates were put through the rituals, sworn to secrecy with terrifying oaths, given a certain amount of occult teaching, most of it easily obtainable from printed sources, and then left to their own devices; one of them complained that he had been told that he was about to be given arcane teachings, had been sworn to silence – and had then had the letters of the Hebrew alphabet confided to his safe-keeping.

In 1892 this neglect of practical work came to an end when MacGregor Mathers added a great deal of material dealing with the techniques of ceremonial magic onto the syllabus studied by the Golden Dawn members.

This came about because in the previous year Westcott had suddenly announced that his correspondence with Anna Sprengel, the German Rosicrucian adept, had ceased. He stated that he had received a letter from Nuremberg informing him that Fraulein Sprengel was dead, that her fellow adepts had disapproved of her teaching activities and of her issuing a charter authorising the foundation of an English temple, that no further instructions or help could be expected from Germany, and that if the English students wanted to make further progress they would have to establish their own links with the 'Secret Chiefs', or 'Masters', the superhuman beings who were the real force behind all authentic occult fraternities.

There is no doubt that Westcott was lying. His correspondence with 'Anna Sprengel' had *not* ceased – for the very simple reason that it had never begun. As Mr. Ellic Howe has proved on the basis of a detailed examination of the supposed 'letters from a German Rosicrucian' they are obvious forgeries, clearly the products of someone who was only poorly acquainted with the language in which they were written. It is impossible to come to any other conclusion than that Wynn Westcott procured their forgery to serve his own ends. This fact does not, of course, prove that the cipher manuscript, with its skeletonic 'magical rituals', was also a forgery – but it does throw a strong suspicion on that document's origins and validity.

Mathers was not dismayed by the (supposedly) sudden isolation of the Golden Dawn. He determined to make his own link with the invisible Masters and eventually, in 1892, with the aid of his wife Moina – the sister of Bergson, the vitalist philosopher – came to believe that he had successfully done so. He has left us his own description of his contact with the Secret Chiefs and the methods by which their wisdom was conferred upon him:

> . . . . it was found absolutely and imperatively necessary that there should be some eminent member especially chosen to act as the link between the Secret Chiefs and the more external forms of the Order. It was requisite that such a member should be me, who, while having the necessary and peculiar basis of critical and profound Occult Archaeological knowledge should at the same time be not only ready but willing to devote himself in every sense to a blind and unreasoning obedience to those Secret Chiefs. . . .
>
> Concerning the Secret Chiefs of the Order, to whom I make reference and from whom I have received the wisdom . . . which I have communicated to you, I can tell you nothing. I know not even their earthly names. I know them only by certain secret mottoes. I have but very rarely seen them in the physical body; and on such rare occasions *the rendez-vous was made astrally by them*. They met me in the flesh at the time and place appointed beforehand. For my part I believe them to be human and living on this earth; but possessing terrible superhuman powers.
>
> When such rendez-vous has been in a much frequented place there has been nothing in their personal appearance or dress to make them out as differing in any way from ordinary people except the appearance

and sensation of transcendent health and vigour (whether they seemed persons in youth or age) which was their invariable accompaniment; in other words the physical appearance which the possession of the Elixir of Life has traditionally been supposed to confer.

On the other hand when the rendez-vous has been in a place free from any access by the Outer World they have usually been in symbolic robes and insignia.

But my physical intercourse with them on these rare occasions has shown me how difficult it is for a Mortal, even though advanced in Occultism, to support the presence of an Adept in the physical body . . . I do not mean that in such rare cases of physical converse with them that the effect produced on me was that intense physical exhaustion which follows depletion of magnetism; but, on the contrary, the sensation was that of being in contact with so terrible a force that I can only compare it to the continued effect of that usually experienced momentarily by any person close to whom a flash of lightning passes during a violent storm; coupled with a difficulty in respiration similar to the half-strangling effect produced by ether; and if such was the result produced on one tested as I have been in Occult work, I cannot conceive a much less advanced Initiate being able to support such a strain, even for five minutes, without death ensuing.

Almost the whole of the . . . Knowledge has been obtained by me from them [i.e. the Secret Chiefs] in various ways, by clairvoyance – by astral projection on their part and mine – by the table, by the ring and disc – at times by Direct Voice audible to my ears and those of Vestigia [Vestigia was the magical motto of Mathers' wife Moina] – at times copied from books brought before me, I know not how – and which disappeared from my vision when the transcription was finished – at times by appointment *astrally* at a certain place, till then unknown to me; an appointment made in the same manner and kept in the same manner as in the case of those rare occasions when I have met them by appointment in the physical body.

The strain of such labour . . . I thought would have killed me or Vestigia, or both, the nerve prostration after each reception being terrible from the strain of testing the correctness of every passage thus communicated; the nerve prostration alluded to, being at the same time accompanied by profuse cold perspirations, and by severe loss of blood from the nose, mouth and occasionally the ears.

You know the extreme and sustained attention and critical judgment requisite . . . Add to all this the Ceremonies of Evocation, almost constant strife with opposing Demonic Forces endeavouring to stop the delivery and reception of the Wisdom, and the necessity of keeping the mind exalted toward the Higher Self . . .

The 'table' and the 'ring and disc', which Mathers mentioned as being two of the methods used by the Secret Chiefs to communicate with him, were adaptations of fairly commonplace spiritualist techniques. The table was just that – a table which rocked about, supposedly at the command of the superhuman Masters, the raps made in the course of its gyrations spelling out messages in a simple code. The ring was of cardboard, painted in symbolic colours. Mathers held it by a silken ribbon, and it swayed about – in precisely the same manner as the swinging pendulum of a dowser – over a disc on which were inscribed Hebrew Letters and mystic symbols. As the ring twisted about the letters and symbols it indicated by its movements meaningful combinations of these.

Such then, were the processes by which Mathers and his wife obtained their magical lore from the Secret Chiefs. Whether these latter had, or have, any objective existence is neither here nor there. The essential thing was that, on the basis of the knowledge that they believed they had obtained from these Masters, the two seers created a complex synthetic occult system which transformed the

Golden Dawn from one of a large number of quasi-masonic secret societies into an association seriously engaged in the practise of ritual magic. The exact nature of that magic – the Mathers' version of the European esoteric tradition – is described in our next chapter.

7 *Fountain of Magic*

Mathers grafted the magical system he had derived from the invisible Secret Chiefs onto the five initiation ceremonies of the cipher manuscripts; these were left unrevised, although a new interpretation was given to them, and the would-be adept had to go through all of them before he was initiated into the Second Order, a body established by Mathers in 1892, and allowed to practise magic.

The first of the rituals taken from the cipher manuscript, that of Neophyte, was simple in form. It bore a certain resemblance to some masonic ceremonies. The candidate, blindfolded, clad in a black robe with a rope tied round his waist was led into the 'Hall of the Neophytes' – a hired room at Mark Masons Hall. After he had been submitted to purification by water, a ritual sprinkling by one of those officiating at the ceremony, and consecration by fire (i.e. the smoke of incense) he was led to a cubical altar, its height that of the navel of a six-foot man, in the centre of the Hall. His hand was placed on the white triangle, symbolic of Divine Light, that lay on the altar together with a blood-red Calvary Cross. Still blindfolded he took an oath binding himself to secrecy and 'to persevere with courage and determination through the labours of the Divine Science, even as I shall persevere . . . through this Ceremony . . . and I will not debase my mystical knowledge in the labour of Evil Magic'.

The taking of the oath was followed by various circumambulations of the Hall and further purifications and consecrations, after which the Hierophant – the Chief

Officer of the Ceremony – invoked the 'Lord of the Universe' over the kneeling candidate. The invocation concluded with the Hierophant addressing the candidate:

> Child of Earth, long hast thou dwelt in Darkness –
> Quit the Night and seek the Day

Simultaneously the blindfold was removed and the candidate was ceremonially received as a Neophyte of the Order. After he had been given various simple occult teachings, mostly rather obvious explanations of the symbolism of the ceremony he had just undergone, the rite concluded with 'the Eucharist of the Four Elements' – all present, one by one, inhaled the perfume of a rose, to represent Air, warmed their hands over a lamp, thus partaking of 'Elemental Fire', ate bread and salt, symbolising Earth, and, finally, drank wine – elemental water.

We have described this ceremony in some detail because in spite of its simple form Mathers came to attach great significance to it and to develop and extend its formulae to such diverse operations as the evocation of spirits, the consecration of talismans, and alchemical transmutation. The manuscript describing these processes was known as Z2 and was one of those that Mathers had obtained from the Secret Chiefs 'by ring and disc'.

The next four rituals were taken, like that of the Neophyte, from the cipher manuscripts and they were attributed to, respectively, Earth, the Moon and Air, Mercury and Water and Venus and Fire. The ceremonies in question were designed to equilibriate in the mind of the candidate the factors symbolised by the Four Elements and were consequently known as the Elemental Grades; one modern authority has referred to them as being 'a sort of ceremonial psychoanalysis combined with a crash-course in occult theory'.

After the Elemental Grades had been taken, a period of seven months – referred to in the Order as 'the regimen of the Planets' – had to elapse before the candidate was allowed to take the Portal Grade, an intermediate degree dividing the Outer Order, the Golden Dawn proper, from the Second Order, in which magic was practised as well as preached. A further nine months usually went by – the analogy to gestation is apparent – before reception into the Second Order, or, to give it its full name, the *Rosae Rubeae et Aureae Crucis,* the Red Rose and Golden Cross. During the waiting period the aspirant was supposed to devote much of his time to an introspective process of self-analysis described as follows:-

> The Aspirant . . . must acknowledge his debt to evolution through which has been perfected the instrument wherein his mind works and gathers material. Then, through meditation he is led to see himself as not only self conscious – as one who receives impressions – one who criticises and watches . . . but, standing outside himself, he now becomes one who endeavours to sense how his mask appears to others – sees himself as part of the consciousness of others, as one who impresses, one who is criticized and watched. . . .
>
> He will reflect on words and the power of words . . . the magic, both good and evil, of human communion by words, he will begin to grasp why the Order reiterates the importance of silence. The true Magician must understand his tools and, in periods of silence, he must contemplate words as one of them.[1]

A second aspect of this interior psycho-therapeutic work was the performance of the 'Middle Pillar Exercise'. This technique involved the frequent visualisation of a stream of psychic energy, imagined as a current of white light, travelling from above the head to the soles of the feet and back again, in the course of its journey vivifying certain centres of energy, sometimes called *chakras*, which were considered not physical (although they were believed to have glandular analogues) but psycho-spiritual, a subtle equivalent of the nervous system.

The use of the Middle Pillar technique was believed to help the body as well as the soul. It was claimed that the regular performance of the exercise not only opened the subtler vehicles of consciousness to beneficent influences but led to good health and an influx of physical energy. It is still widely used by contemporary magicians and is held in high esteem by many of them; Dr. Israel Regardie, for example, has testified to its therapeutic value and has written a short study, *The Art of True Healing*, in which he has outlined an adaptation of the Middle Pillar exercise which allows the experienced practitioner to apply it to others as well as to himself.

At first sight an idea of this type – that a visualisation/meditational system can affect the physical as well as the psychological well-being of its user – seems unworthy of serious consideration. It is worth remarking, however, that it is in conformity with the purely empirical conclusions reached by some American and British physicians regarding the value of psychological exercises as a therapy in cases of cancer. The method taught by these physicians to their patients involves imagining the neoplasm as an invading 'cauliflower' or 'fungus' and the body's defences as rays of brilliant and purifying light fighting against the intruder. This therapy is, of course, a highly unorthodox one, but a small minority of cancer specialists consider it as, at the very least, a useful adjunct to surgery and chemotherapy.

In addition to the work described above the Portal initiate had to study the tarot cards, to pass a simple examination in their use as a means of divination, and to show that he was able to cast a horoscope – that is, to indicate the position of the planets on a geocentric map of the heavens. This done, and the nine months' waiting period having expired, the candidate was admitted to the Second Order by means of the Adeptus Minor ritual.

The ceremony, supplied by one of Mathers' astral contacts was a magnificent piece of theatre, if nothing else. It began with the candidate entering the Temple clad in the impressive robes and regalia of the Portal Grade, bearing a certificate that he had passed the required examination, and demanding his 'reception and acknowledgment as an Adeptus Minor . . . of the Second Order'. He was immediately contemptuously dismissed with the information that: 'It is not by the proclamation of honours and dignities, great though they may be, that thou canst gain admission to the Tomb of the Adepti of the Red Rose and the Cross of Gold'.

After this rejection the crestfallen candidate was taken out, stripped of his vestments and ornaments and made to don a simple black gown. Dressed thus, his hands tied behind his back, he was taken back into the Temple and tied to a large Cross; on this he took the oath of an Adeptus Minor – very similar in its wording to the oath of the composite Secret Rose which we have included in our first chapter.

This concluded, two of the three Adepti who conducted the initiation recited the legend of the finding of the tomb of the mythical occultist Christian Rosycross. As the tale reached its dramatic climax with the words '. . . Frater N.N. threw open the door of the Vault', a door was thrown open and a replica of the original tomb was displayed.

The candidate saw before him a seven-sided Vault, each side divided into forty squares, each square inscribed with a mystic symbol and painted in a different colour – a mosaic of flashing coloured light. In the centre of the Vault lay a coffin, the Pastos of Christian Rosycross, its sides painted with the twelve signs of the zodiac, the seven planets and the elements; at its head a Rose Cross of forty-nine petals, at its foot a white Calvary Cross with a black background.

Within the Pastos lay the Chief Adept, dressed in full regalia, his eyes closed as though in death, his hands crossed upon his breast and clasped in them the Crook and Scourge of the Egyptian god Osiris. Only his head and arms were visible, for over the coffin lay a circular altar painted with various symbolic pictures and upon it a dagger, a goblet, a chain, and a Rose Cross.

The candidate, who had already been handed the magnificently decorated wand of the Chief Adept, was instructed to touch it to the breast of the form that lay before him. He did so and then, without opening his eyes, the Chief Adept spoke a few simple sentences summing up the intended purpose of the ritual:

> Buried with that Light in a mystical death, rising again in a mystical resurrection, cleansed and purified through Him our Master, O Brother of the Cross and the Rose. Like him, O Adepts of the Ages, have ye toiled. Like him ye have suffered tribulation. Poverty, torture and death have ye passed through. They have been but the purification of the gold. In the alembic of thy heart, through the athanor of affliction, seek thou the Stone of the Wise.

This was the high point of the ceremony, although a good deal of explanation of the symbolism of the Vault was still to follow.

The attainment of the Adeptus Minor grade was the beginning of a process, not the conclusion of one; the initiate now began his serious magical work. His first task was the preparation of the implements he would use in the performance of his rites; a Lotus Wand, signifying the twelve signs of the zodiac and the triumph of spirit over matter, a magical sword, symbolising the force and power of Mars, a Rose Cross, a magnificently coloured emblem designed to be worn on the breast of the initiate, and the four 'Elemental Weapons' – a cup for Water, pantacle (or disc) for Earth, a dagger for Air and a wand for Fire. Save for the dagger and the sword all these had to be manufactured by the Adept himself. They were also 'consecrated' by him in a series of magical ceremonies carried out under the supervision of one of the Chiefs of his Temple.

After this making and consecration the initiate moved on to such advanced studies as Enochian and Talismanic magic. In the latter he had to 'gather names, sigils etc. for a Talisman for a special purpose. Make a design for both sides of it – make a special ritual for consecrating to the purpose you have in mind and arrange a time with the Chief for the ceremony of consecration.' In Enochian magic the Adept was instructed to 'make and colour a pyramid for a selected square, and to make the God-form and Sphinx suitable to it . . . prepare a ritual for practical use with this square, and in the presence of a Chief . . . build it up astrally and describe the vision produced.'

This building up of 'astral forms' and the exploration of the astral plane by what was technically known as 'skrying in the spirit-vision' were major parts of the occult activities of the Adept Minor. The 'spirit-vision' achieved, and to which great importance was attached, was no more than an elaborate version of the 'astral projection' which we have described earlier on. All that those who devoted much of their time to astral journeys can *definitely* be said to have attained to was an introspective state in which they experienced vivid, lucid, and internally coherent day-dreams. As for 'building up astral forms', this was merely an extension of the vizualisation techniques used in the exercises of the Middle Pillar.

Initiates were instructed to devise their own magical ceremonies for particular purposes and many did so. Thus, for example, Aleister Crowley wrote rituals to consecrate a Talisman of Jupiter (designed to heal the mother of a friend) and to invoke the demon Buer to visible appearance. The first was completely unsuccessful – because, so Crowley said, its recipient had failed to obey his injunction to water it with dew – the second only partially so; Crowley succeeded in materializing the demon's boot and helmet.

These Crowleyan rituals were complex in the extreme. Far more typical was the ceremony improvised by J.W. Brodie-Innes to destroy 'a vampirising entity' which he believed was obsessing his wife and himself; after burning incense on a coal from his fire, drawing a pentagram in the air with his hand and 'vibrating the Name of Power Adonai-ha Aretz' he saw what he described as a vague blot, like a scrap of London fog, materialise before him. The blot thickened and he saw with complete clarity 'a most foul shape, between a big bellied toad and a malicious ape'. Upon it he astrally projected (i.e. he visualised) a glowing ball of force; there was 'a slight feeling of shock, a foul smell, a momentary dimness, and then the thing was gone'.

Some idea of the complexity of the studies and practical work engaged in by the Adepti Minores can be gained from the syllabus drawn up by Mathers and Westcott for the use of the more senior members of the grade. First of all each one of them had to manufacture a ring and disc of the sort used by Mathers to obtain messages from the Secret Chiefs. This was to be used 'in Divination and Consultation' and was to be worn by the Adept 'suspended from a Ribbon of one, or all, the colours of Malkuth'. After he or she had made and, presumably, consecrated ring and disc the following subjects were included in a list of those to be 'studied and practised':

1) . . . the Symbolism contained in the Zelator Ritual of the First Order . . .
2) Development of the Sense of Clairaudience in the Spirit Vision. [i.e. the seer, when astrally projecting, should hear voices as well as see three-dimensional pictures.]
3) The Knowledge of the Ritual of the Twelve Gates. . . .
4) The method of bringing the Divine White Brilliance into action by a certain Ritual. . . .
7) Of the combination of divers Forces so as to reconcile their action in the same Symbol of Telesma. [This was an aspect of talismanic magic.]
8) The Egyptian Art . . . of a continuous Prayer or Invocation for the Power desired.
9) The Knowledge of ShDIALChI or the Art of taking, in any working, the God Form which would govern the same. . . .
12) Tarot Divination translated into Magical Action.
13) The Knowledge of the Secret Ritual of the symbolism of the order of the Days of the Week of Creation. . . .
15) The opening of the Knowledge of the Masculine and Feminine Potencies necessary unto the mani-

festation of all things symbolised in the diagram of the Flaming Sword between Metatron and Sandalphon. [Metatron and Sandalphon are the Archangels who stand at, respectively, the crown and the foot of the qabalistic Tree of Life.]

Manuscripts on all these aspects of occult lore were circulated privately amongst the Adepti together with other obscure tractates. Considered by many initiates to be the most important of the latter was the document called Z2 to which we have previously referred. This gave the formulae to be employed in various practical workings, amongst them the manufacture of 'an astral shroud of darkness' – i.e. the achievement of invisibility.

Z2, together with much other instructional material concerning ceremonial magic, was published by Dr. Israel Regardie in his excellent *Golden Dawn*, a four-volume work to which we happily refer those of our readers who hanker after evocations, consecrations, and even alchemical transmutations.

Certainly such matters appealed to some Victorian occultists, for by 1899 somewhere between two and three hundred men and women had accepted invitations to be initiated into the order. Over one hundred of these had worked sufficiently hard at the prescribed course of study to have reached the grade of Adeptus Minor and besides the original London temple there were daughter-groups in Bradford, Edinburgh, Weston-super-Mare, and Paris. Of these the most important were the Amen-Ra temple in Edinburgh and the Ahathoor temple in Paris, this last being under the personal direction of Mathers, who had moved to France in 1894, and including amongst its initiates Dr. Encausse ('Papus'), the French magician whose activities were mentioned in an earlier chapter.

It must be admitted that many of those initiated into the order were, by worldy standards, complete nonentities. It is likely that at least some of these were inadequate personalities who sought to compensate for feelings of self-inferiority by acting out fantasies of adeptship; such people have been the bane of modern occult groups, carrying out an absolute minimum of the work prescribed but devoting much time and effort to 'esoteric' gossip and backbiting.

Nevertheless, the Golden Dawn included amongst its membership a number of fascinating personalities, some of them, like Aleister Crowley, destined for notoriety, others, like Arthur Machen, for literary eminence. It is worth taking a brief look at some of the men and women who joined the Golden Dawn in its early years, for the diversity of their characters, opinions and ways of living not only illustrates the way in which the Golden Dawn appealed to men and women who had little in common with one another save an interest in the occult, but partially explains the tensions that were eventually to rip the order apart into a number of competing schisms.

Arthur Machen was one of that minority of Golden Dawn initiates – Oscar Wilde's wife was another – who found the Golden Dawn not to their taste and, a year or two after admission, let their membership lapse.

Machen's objections to the order, its teachings, and the collective ceremonies in which its members engaged themselves, were based on a rejection of its claim to historical links with the alchemical and Rosicrucian adepts of past centuries. Clearly, he argued, the Golden Dawn could not be an ancient foundation, for its 'theology' and the symbolism of the rites expressing that same 'theology', were essentially syncretistic – that is to say, symbolic structures drawn from such diverse sources as the Old Testament, mediaeval sorcery, ancient Egyptian religion, and even modern Hinduism, were blurred and blended into one great mishmash of myth, legend and symbol. The intellectual attitudes which underlay such syncretism were, affirmed Machen, totally alien to any period before the second half of the nineteenth century, and therefore the Golden Dawn was of recent origin and its claims to antiquity totally fraudulent.

There is no doubt that Machen overstated his case. Similar syncretistic leanings can be discerned in some late classical philosophers, such as Iamblichus, in the renaissance – a mosaic of 'Thrice Greatest Hermes' is a feature of one Italian cathedral – and in the 'occult freemasonry' of eighteenth century France and Germany. Nevertheless, coming from Machen this was a damning criticism, for he was favourably disposed towards magic by inclination and, indeed, seems to have had an intuitive understanding of the ideology of that art prior to coming into direct contact with it. For in short stories written over five years *before* his admission into the Golden Dawn he expressed concepts which initiates of that order only came to believe as the result of much astral travel, meditation and ritual workings.

Thus in the novels *Moonchild* and *The Devil's Mistress*, written by, respectively, Aleister Crowley and J.W. Brodie-Innes, there are given (in fictional form) astral, magical interpretations of witchcraft and its connections with evil, repressed sexuality, the Great God Pan ('the Devil') and human atavism – the reversion of mind and protoplasm to earlier forms. These interpretations would seem to have been derived from the Golden Dawn, of which both authors were high-grade initiates, for they seem to be implicit in Mathers' teachings concerning the qlipoth, the evil and averse aspects of the qabalistic Tree of Life of which 'it is dangerous even to think'.

But in Machen's short novel *The Great God Pan* – first published in 1894 and denounced in the *Manchester Guardian* as 'the most acutely and intentionally disagreeable we have yet seen in English' – very similar ideas were expressed quite independently of any Golden Dawn influence. This work recounts, in episodic form, the life of Helen Vaughan, a sort of congenital witch – she is literally a child of Pan – who destroys, both physically and morally, those with whom she comes into close relationships. Her unpleasant career ends with her suicide and atavistic reversion to primal slime; 'I saw the beast descend to the beast whence it descended,' says a witness present at these events.

The *Novel of the White Powder*, a short story incorporated into Machen's episodic novel entitled *The Three Impostors*, also features primal atavism. This time the protagonist is innocent enough, a young man named Francis Leicester who has a tonic prescribed for him by his physician. The pharmacist who makes up the prescription is old, and so are his stocks. Over the years a natural but sinister alchemy has transmuted the harmless tonic into the raw ingredient of *Vinum Sabbati*, the evil brew supposedly drunk by witches in order to revert to more primitive evolutionary forms. The young man's innocence does not save him; the 'Sabbath Wine' destroys first his moral standards and then his physical being, he degenerates into a pool of loathsome black deliquescence which drips through the floor of his room into that which lies below . . .

Apart from his capacity to intuitively arrive at magical concepts Machen seems to have possessed what has been called 'the soul of a natural magician'. In other words, he was one of those rare individuals who have an instinctive capacity to improvise effective occult techniques.

The effect of one such improvisation, which he applied in the autumn of 1899 – *before* his entry into the *Golden Dawn* – impressed him enormously. He wrote about it to a correspondent, the French writer P.J. Toulet, telling him that, while he did not believe in the literal possibility of the events described in *Novel of The White Powder*, experiences he had recently undergone had convinced him that 'we live in a world of great mysteries, of things stupefying and unsuspected.' Elsewhere he described the experiences as a transformation of the everyday world of Victorian London into mystic wonder, 'the merging of Syon into Baghdad'.

It is perhaps significant that Machen discovered his technique shortly after his wife had died, and when he was suffering from acute depression. He was 'beside himself with dismay and torment', he 'could not endure his own being'; then a process suggested itself to him and he 'did what had to be done'. The nature of this process is uncertain and Machen always refused to give details. He

S. L. MacGregor Mathers (1854–1918), the magician from whom many of the occult teachings and techniques used by the Order of the Golden Dawn derived.

did, however, give one hint when he said that 'It would be of no use to me now. . . . Those who desire a hidden life must abstain from many things in common life which are in themselves innocent.'

When Machen wrote the above passage he was happily married to his second wife, when he discovered his process he was an unhappy widower; it is difficult to avoid the conclusion that the technique was in some way sexual in its nature and marital intercourse would have been an obstacle to its performance.

Machen had been brought into the order by A.E. Waite, a writer on mysticism, Rosicrucianism and magic whose early books were published, like Machen's, by George Redway, a splendid rogue who, besides engaging in occult publishing, ran a successful but discreetly conducted pornographic lending library and was once saved from a conviction for fraud by the main prosecution witness against him dropping dead on the day of the hearing.

It was rather surprising that Waite ever bothered to join the Golden Dawn, for he disliked both Mathers and Westcott, describing the latter as 'hooting like some owl nesting in the cypresses beside the tombs of false adepts' and the former as 'a combination of Don Quixote and Hudibras'. Waite had an acid pen but was sugary enough in the flesh. He was probably the most respectable man ever to have engaged in magical pursuits; the only vice he ever seems to have been accused of was an inordinate fondness for *Horlick's Malted Milk*.

W.B. Yeats was the most distinguished man of letters who drew inspiration from the Golden Dawn. He had been introduced to the order by Mathers, who had first met him either in the reading room of the British Museum (as Yeats himself claimed) or, more probably, at Madame Blavatsky's home in Holland Park. He was initiated into the Neophyte grade as early as March 1890, but his occult progress seems to have been uncommonly slow and he showed little magical talent – indeed, over ten years after his initiation it was alleged that he had not even consecrated his 'implements', the magical weapons mentioned earlier.

Whatever Yeats' failings as a magician his membership of the Order did at least enable him to satisfy his desires to pose as an expert in Black Magic – for, like Lionel Johnson and many other of his contemporaries, he displayed an almost adolescent interest in the more erotic components of diabolism. He was a friend of that syphilitic, homosexual devil-worshipper Count Stenbock; he associated himself with the childish antics of a group of Irish clerks who sought to raise the Devil over a bowl of animal blood in a Dublin back-room; he took as his magical motto *Daemon est Deus Inversus* (the Devil is the Reverse Side of God); worst of all he bored Aubrey Beardsley by going on, and on, and on . . . about diabolism, which he seems to have pronounced (according to Max Beerbohm's amusing account of the dinner at which Yeats delivered his monologue) as 'Dyahbolism'.

No personality could have contrasted more with that of Yeats than that of another early member, the Rev. W.A. Ayton, an Oxfordshire vicar. Already an old man when he had first joined the Order, he combined alchemical interests, a considerable knowledge of the literature of occultism and a belief that Mr. Gladstone was a Black Magician and/or a Jesuit in disguise with a great fear of evil spirits. 'Never invoke the spirits,' he urged Yeats, 'even the Olympic Planetary Spirits turn against us in the end.' He was greatly interested in his own health, grew medicinal herbs in a small garden he fertilized with household slops, and inflicted herbal remedies of his own manufacture upon his parishioners.

Ayton dabbled in eccentric theories and was prepared to give credence to anything if it was sufficiently unlikely. He asserted that all pre-Reformation monasteries had been centres of alchemical and magical research and that the truths of occultism were to be found in Gothic wallpaintings, carvings, architecture and stained glass.

He experimented with practical alchemy, complaining bitterly to his stockbroker of the difficulties he experienced with the flues of the stove he used to heat his preparations and fussing about whether or not to buy a platinum crucible. His great ambition was to discover the Elixir of Life; according to one report he eventually did so, but the liquid proved so volatile that it evaporated before he had time to drink it . . .

Another devotee of fringe medicine was a younger and more active member of the order, Edward Berridge, a homoeopathic physician who combined an almost fanatical loyalty to Mathers and his system with the practice of mesmerism and adherence to the strange philosophy (it mixed up unorthodox sexual teachings with deep breathing) of Thomas Lake Harris. Berridge was always trying to convert other members of the Order to the sexual-pneumatic doctrines of Harris by sending them pamphlets through the post.

But unquestionably the most remarkable of the younger members of the order – from, at any rate, the magical point of view, was Aleister Crowley. He had been born in 1875 of middle-class parentage. Both his father and mother were members of the 'closed brethren', the most extreme wing of the fundamentalist Plymouth Brethren, and he was brought up to believe in death, judgment, hell, and the full inspiration of the Bible. At the age of eleven, shortly after the death of his father, he rebelled against this gloomy faith and within a few years had managed by his behaviour to convince his mother that he was the Beast 666 of the Apocalypse.

After a school career much interrupted by illness, some of it self-inflicted (he had to leave one public school because he was suffering from gonorrhoea), and a brief period at the University of London, he went up to Trinity College, Cambridge. Here he settled down to serious study of chess, poetry, erotica, mountain climbing, and almost anything else that came to his attention.

While at Cambridge two things of particular significance happened to Crowley. Firstly, he became aware of a homosexual component in his own nature and had a violent love-affair with a female impersonator named

H.J. Pollit. Secondly, and of greater significance, he began to read the literature of occultism. Among the many books he read was A.E. Waite's compilation *The Book of Black Magic and Pacts* and he was particularly struck by a passage in which Waite hinted that he knew of a certain 'Secret Sanctuary of Adepts'. If there was such a secret sanctuary, Crowley wanted to be part of it, so he wrote to Waite asking how admission could be obtained. He received a kindly reply urging prayer, purity, and the study of *The Cloud on the Sanctuary*, an 18th century mystical work. Whether or not Crowley managed either the prayer or the purity, he certainly read *The Cloud on the Sanctuary* and, for good measure, began to study the writings of the alchemists. Subsequently, while on holiday in Switzerland, he met a young man named Julian Baker, by profession an industrial chemist. Baker, like Crowley, was a student of alchemy and much to Crowley's surprise, seemed to know more about the subject than Crowley himself. 'Was Mr. Baker,' asked Crowley, 'an Adept?' Mr. Baker replied that he was not but that on their return to England he could introduce him to one who was.

The introduction was made, the alleged Adept being George Cecil Jones, another industrial chemist, a resident of Basingstoke in Hampshire, and an Adeptus Minor of the Golden Dawn. Jones put forward Crowley as a suitable candidate for membership of the order and the latter was initiated as a Neophyte in November 1898.

At first Crowley was disappointed with the order, for while he admired the Neophyte ceremony he found his fellow members unimpressive and the teaching he was given to be ludicrously elementary. He was on the point of resignation but Jones persuaded him that he was in no position to judge the order system as a whole until he had reached the Second Order and the grade of Adeptus Minor. Officially he did this eighteen months later, but long before then he had been given copies of almost all the Second Order manuscripts by another member of the order who had become his tutor in magic.

The tutor in question was Alan Bennett – Frater *Iehi*

Aour of the Golden Dawn. Bennett had been born a Catholic but had lost his faith when he had discovered the physiological facts of sex; he regarded the mechanism of human reproduction as so revolting that he could not reconcile its existence with that of a beneficent God. He was by profession an engineer, he suffered, like Crowley, from asthma, and he lived in miserable South London lodgings which he shared with Charles Rosher. Rosher was an occultist whose peculiar career had included a brief tenure of the office of Court Painter to the Sultan of Morocco and the invention of a new and supposedly improved water closet; according to one report this latter was equipped with a flush of such intensity that many mistook the entire apparatus for an eccentric variety of shower-bath.

Bennett had first introduced himself to Crowley by walking up to him and accusing him of meddling with the Goetia (i.e. Black Magic). Crowley had indignantly denied the charge. 'In that case,' Bennett had replied, 'the Goetia has been meddling with you.' Crowley was impressed by this discernment – for he had already decided on the basis of an improbable story told to him by the artist Althea Gyles, that W.B. Yeats, jealous of his poetic abilities, was using Black Magic against him – and by the tales he had heard of Bennett's magical powers; that, for example, Bennett owned a magically charged glass lustre (a prismatic length of glass from a chandelier) with which he had once paralysed for fourteen hours a sceptical Theosophist who had doubted its powers.

At Crowley's invitation Bennett moved into the former's Chancery Lane apartment and there the two began to go on astral journeys together, to invoke spirits, including the goetic demons, and to experiment with substances that would 'loosen the girders of the soul'; that is to say, they took hallucinogenic drugs.

In view of Crowley's later notoriety as a drug addict it is worth saying that it would seem to have been Bennett who introduced him to drugs and not vice versa. For Bennett had been interested in plant-substances alleged to produce clairvoyance for some considerable time and in a letter written in about 1894 to F.L. Gardner – the same magician-stockbroker who had had to endure the Rev. W.A. Ayton's grumblings about his alchemical stove – he went on at some length about the vision-inducing properties of a plant which he referred to as *Dictamnus Fraxinella Alba*. This plant is usually called *Dictamnus Alba (Dictamnus Fraxinella* is an alternative name) and is more familiarly known to present-day gardeners as 'gas plant' or 'burning bush plant'. Magicians refer to it as Dittany of Crete, Aleister Crowley affirmed that the smoke from its burning was the ideal medium for inducing demons to take on visible form, and the Zoroastrian fire-worshippers of India regard it as sacred.

In spite of the interest Bennett took in it there seems no reason to believe that *D. Alba* has any more visionary properties than most garden plants. Probably Bennett regarded it with some awe for the same reason that has induced Parsees to regard it as holy and English gardeners to call it the gas plant – on still, warm, days it exudes a heavy, volatile substance which lingers around the flowers, can be set on fire, and then burns with a brilliant flame which usually leaves the plant undamaged.

In experimentation with drugs and all other occult pursuits Crowley proved an apt pupil and, while still nominally a member of a very junior grade of the order, achieved a better grasp of the Golden Dawn system than most of those who were supposedly Minor Adepts. In giving Crowley all this teaching Bennett had broken his initiation oath; officially even the existence of the Second Order was supposed to be kept a secret from those outside it. However, it is plain that Bennett had acted with the approval of Mathers who had taken a great liking to Crowley and had come to regard him not only as a follower but as a close personal friend. This friendship was to prove, as will be described in the next chapter, an important factor in the upheavals that led to the destruction of the order in its original form.

8 *Golden Dawn Derivatives*

As was described in the previous chapter the Golden Dawn built up a considerable membership in the years between its foundation and the end of the century. Politically – that is *magically* politically – these years were eventful for the order, for Mathers managed to oust Westcott from his occult dignities and to establish himself as the supreme spiritual and administrative monarch of a shaky esoteric despotism.

Westcott gave up his official position in the order towards the middle of March 1897. His resignation was by no means voluntary, but was forced upon him by the Home Office, who seem to have told him that he was perfectly free to be either a Coroner or one of the leaders of a secret society dedicated to the practice of magic – but not both. Westcott bowed to the official pressures exerted upon him, but most unhappily. He wrote a dejected letter to a fellow-initiate in which he said that he had

> . . . very sadly resigned all my offices in G.D. and remain but a private Adept. I have to say that, as it happens, the reason is a purely personal one, owing to my having received an intimation that it had somehow become known to the State officers that I was a prominent official of a society, in which I had been foolishly posturing as one possessed of magical powers – and if this became more public it would not do for a Coroner of the Crown to be made shame of in such a mad way. So I had no alternative – I cannot think who it is that

> persecutes me. . . . It looks as if someone was trying to get me out of G.D. office – eh?[1]

This letter makes it apparent that Westcott believed that someone had denounced him to the authorities. If this was so it seems likely that this was Mathers, who had been in London only a few days previously. Perhaps, however, Westcott's suspicions were unjustified and, if this was so, there is little reason to doubt a story current in the order at the time. This was, that someone had accidentally left some magical records with Westcott's name upon them in a hansom cab, that these had been handed in by the finder at Scotland Yard, and that in this way the police, and their masters at the Home Office, had become aware of Westcott's supposed adepthood in the magical arts.

Whatever the source of the information about Westcott which reached the Home Office there can be no doubt that the results of it were advantageous to Mathers, making him, in effect, supreme governor of the order. The only other Golden Dawn initiate who might have been a serious potential rival to him was Annie Horniman, the wealthy daughter of a tea merchant, who had entered the order in its early years – she had been the first to have been initiated into the Second Order – and, believed herself to be in communication with a Secret Chief who called himself the Purple Adept. Miss Horniman, however, had been expelled from the order by Mathers some three months or so before Westcott's resignation. Supposedly this was because she had 'raised up dissensions' against Mathers and had continually exhibited 'intense arrogance, narrowness of judgment and self-conceit'. In reality the expulsion was the culmination of a long series of rows between Miss Horniman on one side and Mathers, his wife, and some of his closest associates, on the other. Mathers was not an easy man to get on with – men who believe themselves to be superhuman rarely are – but most of the fault seems to have been on the other side. Thus, for example, Annie Horniman, who was prudish to the point of mania, infuriated Mathers by purporting to discover some sexual impurity in his occult teachings. It is only fair to say that any imputation of this sort was totally unjustified. Mathers' sole sexual irregularity was that which the late Kenneth Tynan described as 'the worst perversion of them all', that is, chastity. Mathers and his wife regarded copulation as an obstacle to spiritual progress and they never consummated their marriage. Moina Mathers wrote 'I think . . . all . . . sexual connections are *beastly*' and, referring to a magical theory concerning sexual relationships between human beings and elemental spirits, she added:

> When I first heard of this theory it gave me a shock, but not such a horrible one as that which I had when I was young, about the human [sexual] connection. . . . I remember that my horror of human beings for a while was so great that I could not look at my own mother without violent dislike and loathing. I have always chosen as well as [my husband] to have nothing whatever to do with any sexual connection – we have both kept perfectly clean I know, as regards the human, the elemental, and any other thing whatever.

With the departure of Annie Horniman and the withdrawal of Westcott into private adeptship – he led a small group which met at his home for the purpose of carrying on astral workings – Mathers became increasingly tyrannical and eccentric. Much to the alarm of many Golden Dawn initiates he began to involve himself with the lunatic fringe of right-wing politics, busying himself with obscure royalist conspiracies and making friends with such human oddities as the Pretender to the throne of Byzantium.

Throughout 1899 Mathers became more and more friendly with Aleister Crowley. This disturbed some members of the order, for they not only looked upon the latter as half-mad but were suspicious, and rightly so, of his sexual tendencies. This disturbance was further increased when Mathers decided to publicly revive the religion of ancient Egypt by hiring a small theatre and invoking the goddess Isis before a paying audience. He seems to have been persuaded into this act of tomfoolery by Jules Bois, the magician/journalist whose involvement with the sinister Boullan has been mentioned earlier.

Mathers played the part of High Priest and his wife that of High Priestess in the ceremony. The Paris correspondent of the *Sunday Chronicle* was impressed by the latter, describing her as having a 'graceful attitude and dignified manner', but not by her husband. Mathers, he wrote, had 'a terrible English accent' and

> He looked for all the world like . . . a Scotchman. And, sure enough, when I made enquiries after the performance, a braw Highlander he proved to be. M'Gregor is his name, but whence he comes I know not. They call him Count M'Gregor in one of the French newspapers, but this, M. Jules Bois says, is a mistake. 'Monsieur M'Gregor is only the chief of an old Scottish clan!'

Towards the end of 1899 the London officers of the Second Order refused Crowley the Adeptus Minor initiation, to which he was formally entitled, because, in the words of one of them, 'a mystical fraternity is not a moral reformatory'. Crowley, angry at this rebuff, hurried off to Paris, where he was sympathetically received by Mathers and given the desired initiation on 16 January 1900.

Mathers' action in initiating one whom they had rejected gave the members of the Second Order no pleasure. They refused to give Crowley official copies of the instructional manuscripts to which he was entitled and at the same time Florence Farr, who had been acting as Mathers' London representative, wrote to Mathers informing him that she no longer wanted to be his lieutenant.

Mathers leapt to quite the wrong conclusion; deciding that Westcott was both trying to make a come-back as magician and to oust him, Mathers, from his position of sole chieftainship, he wrote a strongly worded letter accusing his former friend of forgery:

> . . . . it would be with the very greatest regret . . . that I should receive your resignation . . . but I cannot let you form a combination . . . with the idea of working secretly or avowedly under Sapere Aude [i.e. Westcott] . . .
>
> He has never been at any time in personal or written communication with the Secret Chiefs of the Order, he himself having forged or procured to be forged the professed correspondence between him and them, and my tongue having been tied all these years by a previous Oath of Secrecy to him, from me, before showing me what he had done, or caused to be done, or both. You must comprehend from what little I say here the extreme gravity of such a matter. . . .

In other words Mathers was denying the existence of the supposed correspondence between Westcott and Fraulein Sprengel to which we have previously referred. In spite of this Mathers clearly believed in the real existence of the lady in question, for he concluded his letter by stating that she was with him in Paris. Mathers was greatly mistaken. The woman who was with him and who was posing as Anna Sprengel was in reality an unpleasant occult adventuress named Madame Horos. Eventually, after stealing a set of rituals from Mathers and making a brief visit to South Africa, she set up a bogus Golden Dawn in London at 99 Gower Street – later to be the offices of the *Spectator* – and was finally sentenced to a long term of imprisonment for helping her husband to rape under-age girls.

Florence Farr was extremely upset by Mathers' letter, for she believed in the existence of the Secret Chiefs as deeply and sincerely as a Catholic believes in transubstantiation. After some days thought she wrote to Westcott asking him for his reply to Mathers' charges. The reply she received was curiously diffident; Westcott affirmed that the correspondence with Germany had taken place but said that his witnesses were dead and he would therefore prefer to let the matter drop. It was much too late for that, however. The Second Order had already elected a committee which, on 3 March 1900, wrote to its Chief asking him for proof of the charges of forgery.

A series of angry but futile letters were exchanged between London and Paris and then, at the end of March, the Second Order declared its independence of its creator. Mathers' response to this was a letter affirming his links with the Secret Chiefs and threatening the rebels with the 'punitive current', a sort of magical death-ray.

> I have always acknowledged and shall always maintain the authority of the Secret Chiefs of the Order, to whom and the Eternal Gods I bow, but to none beside!
>
> I know to a nicety the capacities of my human brain and intelligence and what these can of themselves grasp, and I therefore know also when the Forces of the Beyond, and the Presence of the Infinite manifest, and when the Great Adepts of this Planet, the Secret Chiefs of the Order, are with me.
>
> Do you imagine that where such men as Count de Gebelin, Etteila, Christian and Lévi failed in their endeavour to discover the Tarot attributions that I would be able of my own power and intelligence *alone* to lift the veil which has baffled *them*?
>
> . . . I tell you plainly were it possible to remove me from my place as Visible Head of the Order . . . you would find nothing but disruption and trouble fall upon you. . . . And for the first time since I have been connected with the Order I shall formulate my request to the Highest Chiefs for the Punitive Current to be prepared to be directed against those who rebel. . . .

If the fearsome punitive current was switched on it must have been somehow short-circuited, for the rebels were unharmed. Mathers decided to supplement it with more material methods and despatched Crowley to London with instructions to seize the Order's premises and to cow the revolting Adepti.

The arrival of Crowley, regarded by Yeats and others as 'an unspeakable madman', alarmed the rebels and they launched an astral attack upon him. According to Yeats it was completely successful; he claimed that the Order's wonder-workers had 'called up' one of Crowley's mistresses on the astral plane and told her to betray her lover. Two days later, said Yeats, she spontaneously approached a member of the Order and offered to go to Scotland Yard and give evidence of 'torture and medieval iniquity'. Crowley's diary gave quite a different account of this psychic attack – his ornamental Rose Cross turned white, while fires refused to burn in his lodgings; his rubber mackintosh spontaneously went up in flames, for no apparent reason he lost his temper, and on at least five occasions horses bolted at the sight of him.

Crowley replied by seizing the Order's premises with the aid of some toughs he had hired at a pub in Leicester Square; according to one of the rebels Crowley paid them the sum of thirteen shillings and fourpence a day, the face-value of some long-forgotten medieval coin. The triumph was only a temporary one. With the aid of the police the Second Order regained control of its premises and, for good measure, managed to persuade one of Crowley's creditors to issue a writ against him. Crowley had had enough of the struggle and set off for a holiday in Mexico.

While all this was going on in London Mathers was resorting to black magic in Paris. He had taken a large packet of dried peas, baptised each pea with the name of one of his opponents, invoked the devils Beelzebub and Typhon-Set and had then, simultaneously shaking the peas in a large sieve, called upon these dark gods to confound the rebels with quarrels and discord. This seems to have been one of the most successful curses ever recorded, for having got rid of Mathers the members of the Golden Dawn spent the next few years quarrelling violently with one another.

After his Mexican holiday Crowley visited the Far East, principally to see Alan Bennett who had gone to Ceylon and become a Buddhist monk. For a year or two Crowley also became a Buddhist, abandoning the practice of magic and taking up yoga. On his return to Europe he visited Mathers, told him of his yogic exercises and tried to convert him to Buddhism. Mathers expressed his unconcern with both subjects and all Crowley's admiration for him turned to loathing – he alleged that Mathers had stolen a valuable travelling bag from him, had cast an evil spell resulting in the sudden death of his pack of bloodhounds, and had forced Mrs. Mathers to earn a living by prostitution. Whether or not Mathers used black magic against either Crowley or his dogs, there is no doubt that Crowley himself resorted to sorcery against his former Chief. In May 1904 he wrote in his notebook: 'find a man to entrap Mathers. Let him read Lévi then go,' and in the following year he evoked Beelzebub against Mathers and the Golden Dawn; unfortunately only the first page of the ritual he used has survived – the remainder of it was destroyed by Crowley's disciple C.S. Jones – but it seems to have been Crowley's first experiment in hardcore Satanism. It is interesting to note that Crowley's wife Rose, daughter of the Vicar of Camberwell and a sister of a future President of the Royal Academy, participated in the rite, for the rubric describes her as bending over 'arse as high as possible' throughout the ceremony.

By 1908 Crowley had created Magick, his own gnostic system, a blend of Golden Dawn techniques, yogic practices, and the religious theory of the *Book of the Law*, an extraordinarily beautiful prose-poem in three short chapters which he had written down at Cairo in 1904, supposedly at the dictation of a super-human being named Aiwass. By 1912 a fourth component had been added, the sexual magic of the Order of Oriental Templars, a German-based fraternity. This is dealt with in some detail in a later chapter.

While Crowley had been formulating his Magick the Adepti – or, as Crowley referred to them, the Inepti – of the Golden Dawn had split into three competing groups.

The largest of these was the Stella Matutina, the Star of the Morning, led by Dr. R.W. Felkin, an expert in tropical medicine who had been one of the first Christian missionaries in Uganda, had subsequently drifted into occultism, and had finally developed an obsessional desire to establish a direct connection between himself and the Secret Chiefs.

As early as 1902 Felkin came to believe that he had made the sort of contact he so much desired.

The supposed link was astral not physical in nature: the 'Secret Chiefs' communicated with Felkin through the trance mediumship of his wife, giving him much 'advanced teaching' and instructing him to revise the Order's initiation rituals. Felkin was not satisfied with these astral meetings, he wanted to meet the Secret Chiefs in the flesh, and between 1901 and the outbreak of World War I he and his wife made many visits to central Europe in the hope of meeting authentic Rosicrucians. In 1906 he met with his first success, becoming acquainted with 'a professor, his adopted daughter and another gentleman near Hanover . . . undoubtedly Rosicrucians'. He found however that they were secretive and averse to giving him any information because he was neither a freemason nor a member of any occult society that they had knowledge of. This obstacle was removed in the following year when Felkin was made a mason and from then on there was a continual flow of teaching from the German group to the Stella Matutina.

The so-called Rosicrucians whom Felkin had contacted were led by Rudolph Steiner, at the time still chief of the German section of the Theosophical Society. Their activities were secret for the very simple reason that they were operating as an inner ring in the Theosophical Society without either the knowledge or the approval of the Chiefs of that organisation. Subsequently Steiner was to close down his secret society and to abandon the use of ritual; after his death some of his disciples even went as far as to deny that he had ever used ceremonial, but there is hard evidence that his Rosicrucian group existed, that it may well have been a section of the Order of Oriental Templars – an organisation to which we have already referred in connection with Crowley's sexual magic – and that its initiation rituals were a variant form of those used by continental freemasons. An amusing description of Steiner officiating at such an initiation has survived:

> The Temple door opens, you pass in and circumambulate the room three times, sitting down three times, during which the Master of Ceremonies declaims in a religious voice, mysterious and sphinx-like. Then at last you sit down still blindfolded and you feel something happening at your waist and neck. Suddenly the

Aleister Crowley (1875–1947) in magical vestments, before 1914.

bandage is raised by the guide, and you see in front of you a skull which Steiner holds under your noise. Steiner has a server, one on each side – a deacon and vice-deacon – bearers of wax-candles; the whole in dense obscurity. The bandage falls again: after a time it is taken away altogether, you are . . . *Initiated*: you begin to see light. This light comes from wax-candles placed on three altars; black draperies hang everywhere, symbolizing the darkness which is always near. . . . Steiner, the High Priest, is completely clothed in red, with a long Mephistophelian tail and red cap; he is before an altar, in the form of a cube, on which are a crucifix, a cup, and a candle; the two servers, wearing masonic aprons, are before another cube holding candles; the Grand Master of the Ceremonies is near to Steiner. You glance at yourself and see the masonic apron in front with triangle and trowel. You place your hand on the Gospel of St. John; then you are told the password, the apprentice sign, and the sacred name which you can only stammer; it is YAKIM. Then with two extended swords curious signs are made in front of you. Then a sermon from Steiner on the legend of Hiram and Solomon. . . . Then the Repast, during which they look for the underground Temple, the Vault, then being built in Munich. Second address from Steiner, he has taken off the red robe and now wears an alb of lace; he speaks on the Triangle and the eye of God, which is in the centre of the Triangle, and of man's being. Close of the ceremony, which has lasted four hours: ritualistic knocks with mallets on the three cubes; candles extinguished and again lighted, the black draperies of burial are removed; you are surrounded with red bullock's blood; it is the light at last! . . . *Ite missa est*!. . . . You are *Initiated*!

In 1910 Dr. Felkin sent a certain Neville Meakin to Germany as his personal representative; according to the official history of the Stella Matutina this was because Steiner and his Rosicrucians had said 'that in order to form a definite etheric link between themselves and Great Britain it was necessary for a Frater from Great Britain to be under their instruction for a year'.

In the summer of 1912 Felkin and his wife followed Meakin to Germany. During a lengthy stay they visited five Temples and took part in ceremonies which they believed conferred higher magical grades upon them. Felkin himself also seems to have received some sort of unorthodox medical treatment from Steiner – coloured lights were shone upon him while, behind a curtain, unseen 'healing rites' were carried out. At the same time Felkin and Steiner supposedly came to an agreement by which 'anyone . . . who is a full Adeptus Minor . . . may be sent abroad . . . one or more grades may be given him'. This foreign travel was not considered absolutely essential, for Felkin believed that if the 'new methods' (i.e. the mental and physical exercises devised by Steiner) were introduced into the Order its members would progress just as well.

Felkin devised new ceremonies for three new 'high grades' above Adeptus Minor; he constructed them on the basis of what he had seen in Germany padded out by extracts from the Egyptian *Book of the Dead* and *Light on the Path*, an 'inspirational' work produced by a Theosophist named Mabel Collins.

Amongst those who underwent at least one of these 'advanced initiations' was W.B. Yeats, for a document, now in the possession of Senator Michael Yeats, gives a 'clairvoyant description' of the astonishing things that took place on the astral plane during the course of the rite. These involved Yeats's astral body undergoing various odd metamorphoses while his physical body lay motionless in a coffin and a bell was rung thirty-six times:

> At the Sixteenth [ring] he . . . emerges into a further higher plane; at the Seventeenth he is like a transparent rainbow. The Colours of the Planets play upon him. Then they merge into brilliant light and for the rest of the Bells he [i.e. Yeats's astral body] shone with it . . .

In 1912 Dr. and Mrs. Felkin chartered a new Stella Matutina temple situated in New Zealand. Four years later they emigrated to that country. Shortly before this event they set up three new English temples, promulgated a new constitution for the order, and expressed their desire 'that all scattered Rosicrucian forces should be gathered together into an harmonious whole'. In this wish they were to be, as is described in the next chapter, bitterly disappointed.

The second group derived from the original Golden Dawn was the Rosicrucian Order of the Alpha et Omega, usually known as the AO. This was made up of those who had either remained loyal to Mathers throughout the revolt or had decided that they had been wrong to rebel and had returned to their original allegiance. Originally this group had been very small – Mathers' own Parisian temple, a London temple under the leadership of Dr. Berridge, the homoeopath and disciple of Thomas Lake Harris, and some American temples led by individuals initiated by Mathers in his Paris temple prior to 1900. In 1911, however, J.W. Brodie-Innes, one of the more prominent of those who had taken part in the revolt, resumed contact with Mathers. By the summer of the following year he was in a position to tell Felkin that he was getting 'new and exceedingly powerful formulae' from Mathers, and at about the same time he revived the dormant Edinburgh temple of the order. This temple, 'Amen-Ra', was now in possession of instructional documents – the 'new and exceedingly powerful formulae' – not available to Felkin and the Stella Matutina. Brodie-Innes offered copies to Felkin, but on condition 'that you can recognize me as Chief Adept in Anglia, or Scotia . . .'

Felkin enquired what teaching was available and asked for details of the exact nature of the authority which the Scottish magician claimed. Brodie-Innes' reply was very specific:

> I have stacks of MSS and teachings going to far further lengths than I used to think possible. . . . My commis-

> sion as such comes from the Third Order – or, not to make any ambiguity of these words, from those High Adepts whom I so term – and I can pass them on to such as acknowledge my authority and position. This of course involves recognition of Mathers who has committed his authority to me.

By 1914, then, the temple led by Brodie-Innes was also part of the AO.

The only other important Golden Dawn Schism in the period before World War I was a brotherhood led by A.E. Waite and sometimes referred to as the *Holy* Order of the Golden Dawn. Waite used rewritten versions of the Mathers rites, Christianising them and removing – as far as it was possible so to do – the magical elements while emphasising the mystical. Initiates of his temple seem to have rarely, if ever, indulged themselves in either ceremonial magic or astral workings. Two writers of note were initiates of Waite's temple and to some extent fell under the influence of its chief's personal interpretations of magic, the qabalah and the tarot. The first was Charles Williams, the novelist, poet and critic. Williams' novels – notably *The Greater Trumps*, *Many Dimensions* and *Descent Into Hell* – give a Christianised version of much occult theory and Waite's influence is even more apparent in Williams' historical writings such as *Witchcraft* and *Descent of the Dove*. The second of these writers was Evelyn Underhill, author of many popular studies of theology and mysticism. It is perhaps surprising that such a modernist as Evelyn Underhill – she was a friend and correspondent of von Hügel – should have been a member of Waite's temple. But occult traditions have always affirmed that this was the case, and letters, now in the possession of Mr. R. Gilbert and quoted by Evelyn Underhill's most recent biographer, confirm the truth of these traditions.

Beside the three competing fraternities described above there was one important pre-1914 occult grouping which derived many of its practical techniques, for example those employed in the attainment of astral projection, from Mathers and the Golden Dawn. This was the A.A., or Silver Star, founded by Aleister Crowley in 1908. This taught Crowley's Magick and partially abandoned secrecy, actively seeking new members and publishing *The Equinox*, a bulky biennial volume which ran from 1909 to 1913.

9 *Later Occult Brotherhoods*

It will be remembered that before their final departure to New Zealand Dr. and Mrs. Felkin chartered three new temples of the Stella Matutina.

One of these was situated in Bristol and was led by occultists experienced in the Golden Dawn magical tradition, another was intended for freemasons, and the third was A.E. Waite's 'Golden Dawn' which now became part of the Stella Matutina. Felkin instructed that English members of Rudolph Steiner's Anthroposophical Society who wanted to take part in ceremonial magic should be admitted to this temple. The incorporation of Waite's temple into the Stella Matutina took place because Waite had left his own fraternity because of what he called 'internecine feuds over documents'.

Felkin left his own London temple, 'Amoun', under the command of three lieutenants; a Miss Stoddart, who lived at 56 Redcliffe Gardens and established the temple at the same address, and a 'Rev. Will Reason' were two of these. We have been unable to find out anything at all about the second. Supposedly he was an Anglican priest, but, as we have been unable to trace him, we suspect that either he used an alias or his orders were derived from the Protestant Episcopal Church of the USA. In any case he did not long remain as one of the temple chiefs, resigning from his office and being replaced by Dr. W. Hammond, one of the chiefs of the Masonic-Anthroposophical temple mentioned above. The third of the chiefs appointed by Dr. Felkin, and in some ways the most interesting, was the

Rev. Francis Nicholson Heazell. Like Felkin he had a missionary background, having been first a member, and then the head, of the Archbishop of Canterbury's mission to that curious and much-persecuted people, the Assyrian Christians. After his return from the Middle East he had held various curacies and in 1918 was to become Vicar of St. Michael and All Angels, Croydon.

Under its three London chiefs there was none of the 'gathering together of scattered Rosicrucian forces' which the Felkins had wished for. Instead the Stella Matutina was almost destroyed by an obsessive concern with the astral plane and revelations supposedly derived from its inhabitants.

Astral projection and spiritualist-type mediumship had, of course, been quite popular pursuits in the original Golden Dawn and quite a lot of Mathers' teachings had been, as was described earlier, derived from séances with the 'table'. But now they were indulged in almost to the exclusion of all else and the three chiefs, particularly Miss Stoddart, attached great importance to them. They were continually experiencing 'visions of the Secret Chiefs' accompanied by messages about a coming 'Great Initiation'. To prepare for this event Miss Stoddart and her two co-chiefs were instructed to form a 'triangle of power' in order to form a link with the 'hidden Masters'; Miss Stoddart was to be the 'apex of the triangle' and was told that she was to 'shine down the glorious beauty of the Father's face'. She was also to join the Church of England.

She did so, but her experiences during Church services were unusual – she saw visions, underwent trances and received much secret occult teaching[1].

These peculiar religious experiences continued for two years until they reached their high point during an Easter service held in April 1919. Then, in place of the altar, Miss Stoddart saw the 'astral Vault of the Adepti' and, filing into it, twelve hooded, black-robed figures. She experienced a stabbing pain in the region of her heart, felt 'a curious creeping faintness' come over her, and saw a 'dazzling astral fire' over her head. The following day her 'astral master' informed her that she had failed to take the 'Great Initiation' but that this would be given to her some time in the future. By now, however, both she and her fellow-chiefs were thoroughly alarmed; they decided that they were under attack by sinister 'Black Rosicrucians', associated in some way with the German General Staff, who were trying to gain control of their physical bodies. They contacted Felkin in New Zealand, begging for his help. He replied: 'I think it would be better if, instead of fearing imaginary Black Rosicrucians in Germany or elsewhere, you would consciously endeavour to co-operate with the true Rosicrucians who do undoubtedly exist, and are seeking to guide Central European thought into the Light; you would then belong to the Great Work for the World.'

This advice was disregarded and all the Stella Matutina temples were closed down save for the Hermes temple in Bristol and Felkin's own New Zealand temple.

The two male chiefs withdrew into obscurity, but Miss Stoddart went on to fresh triumphs, turning her attention to ultra-right politics and becoming an associate of the late Nesta Webster. The latter, an enthusiastic advocate of the conspiracy theories developed by such early 19th century writers as Robison and Barruel, believed that the French Revolution had been engineered by sinister freemasons and illuminati. Miss Stoddart not only came to share these beliefs but to extend them; all occult secret societies, but particularly the Golden Dawn and the Stella Matutina, were agents of the Jewish conspiracy partially revealed in the *Protocols of the Learned Elders of Zion*. . . .

For many years Miss Stoddart expounded her views in articles regularly published in a notably lunatic anti-semitic sheet called *The Patriot*. The German General Staff and the emerging nationalist parties of the Weimar Republic were revealed, like the Golden Dawn, to be mere agents of the Jewish plan for world domination.

The closure of the majority of its temples did not bring the Stella Matutina to its end. The life of the New Zealand temple founded by Dr. Felkin proved vigorous, and it still flourishes today, so we understand.

No magical fraternity can survive if it becomes totally ossified and inevitably enough 'Smaragdum Thalasses' – as Felkin's New Zealand foundation is named – has been influenced by other occult tendencies than those derived from Mathers and the Golden Dawn. Such influences, we have been told, have included the 'esoteric Christianity' of the German-American occultist Max Heindel and the alchemical magic advocated by 'Frater Albertus' and the Paracelsus Research Society of Salt Lake City.

The Bristol temple also flourished throughout the period 1919–39, but becoming dormant in the early 1940s. A quarter of a century later two temples which claimed to be at least partially derived from this West Country temple were actively using Mathers's system; we are satisfied, however, that their claims to a magical 'apostolic succession' from the Stella Matutina was without foundation.

The temples loyal to MacGregor Mathers – the Alpha et Omega – were subjected to many strains during World War I. Mathers himself found little time to practise or teach magic, for, although accused by Aleister Crowley of being a German agent, he was devoted to France, his adopted country, and he turned his home into a recruiting office for the Foreign Legion. As a result of this those temples under the Brodie-Innes jurisdiction achieved an even greater *de facto* independence than had previously been the case. These temples were not, however, particularly active during the years 1914–18, for most potential recruits were either serving in the armed forces or in such auxiliary organisations as the VAD.

Mathers died in November 1918, a victim of the worldwide epidemic of Spanish influenza. After this the AO became in effect two separate, although allied, magical fraternities, the first conducted by Brodie-Innes, the second by Moina Mathers.

Both these magicians died in the 1920s, but the AO continued with E.J. Langford-Garstin as its most active adept. He eventually committed suicide after meeting with financial disaster and soon afterwards the AO seems to have become dormant.

An occult fraternity which flourished during the years 1918–1939 and had a friendly attitude towards all the groups deriving from the Golden Dawn, but particularly the AO, was the Cromlech Temple.

Membership of this was largely confined to Anglicans and a substantial number – perhaps a majority – of its initiates were Anglo-Catholic clergymen.

The Cromlech Temple was led by a priest possessed of mediumistic abilities who was the recipient of much astral teaching from 'Masters and Guides'.

The aim of the order was 'the establishment of the Kingdom of Love in the heart of Mortal Man', which 'no man can of himself attain', but can be achieved 'through the ministrations of the Higher Adepts who work by the magical powers conferred on them'. The reception of such powers is 'the Supreme Initiation' which in the Church is 'signified by the ordination of the Priesthood, symbolically passing down the magic gifts received from the Master of Masters'. Those who wanted to personally communicate with higher powers were instructed to join the AO:

> If you seek for practical instruction in the Occult Arts or Sciences mentioned in the ritual of this grade, instructions may be obtained through the Society of the Golden and Rosy Cross known as the AO in the Outer. With the knowledge and training obtained in the higher grades thereof it will be possible for each of you, if ye advance far enough, to communicate personally with the Masters of this Order. . . .

The Cromlech Temple became dormant at about the time of the outbreak of World War II, according to one report as a response to an episcopal ultimatum resulting from an enquiry into occult practices engaged in by a number of East Anglican clerics.

There were, of course, numerous occultists who

continued to work at ceremonial magic, sometimes with unfortunate results. One such, an experimenter with the Abramelin techniques we have described in Chapter Three, wrote a letter to the *Occult Review* describing the difficulties he or she had encountered:

> Desiring some information which I could not get in the ordinary way, I resorted to the System of Abramelin, and to this end prepared a copy of the necessary Talisman, perfecting it to the best of my ability with my little stock of knowledge. The ritual performed, I proceeded to clear my place of working. A little knowledge is a dangerous thing; my ritual was imperfect and I only rendered the Talisman useless without in any way impairing the activities of the entity invoked. This looks like nothing else than gross carelessness on my part; and to a certain extent this is true – but the point I wish to make is this, that my knowledge of this particular system, and therefore my ritual, were imperfect; and in any case, I had been shown no method of combating this particular entity when once aroused. Now note the results.
>
> Unfortunately I have no account of the date when these occurrences began, but the first hint of trouble must have come on or about March 3rd 1927. I can guess the date with fair accuracy because, as I was to learn, the manifestations were always strongest about the new moon, and after I had gone to sleep. Upon this occasion I can remember waking up suddenly with a vague feeling of terror oppressing me; yet it was no ordinary nightmare terror, but an imposed emotion that could be thrown off by an effort of the will. This passed almost as soon as I stood up, and I thought no more about it.
>
> Again, on April 2nd or thereabouts, I was troubled by the same feeling, but regarded it as nothing more than a severe nightmare, though the fact that my sleep was distorted towards the time of the new moon had occurred to me; while as full moon drew on, the nights were peaceful again.
>
> The new moon of May 1st brought a recurrence of the

Although Aubrey Beardsley regarded the diabolism affected by some of the minor writers of the 1890s as silly, his genius enabled him to convey the inmost nature of the way of spiritual and intellectual perversity which can lead, through the breaking of taboos, to self-realisation. (Of a Neophyte and how the Black Art was revealed to him by the fiend Asomuel, which appeared in the *Pall Mall Magazine*, June 1893.)

trouble, this time very much more powerful, and necessitated an almost intolerable effort of will to cast it off. Also it was about this time that I first saw the entity which was rapidly obsessing me. It was not altogether unlovely to look at. The eyes were closed and it was bearded with long flowing hair. It seemed a blind force slowly waking to activity.

Now there are three points which I must make quite clear before I proceed. In the first place I was never attacked twice in the same night. Secondly, when I speak of physical happenings, the smashing of glass and voices, they were never, with one absolutely inexplicable exception, actual, but pure illusions; and this leads to the third point. Not one of these incidents happened while I was asleep. Always I found myself awake with the terror upon me and struggling violently to cast off the spell. I have had nightmares before, but no nightmare that I have ever had could hold my mind in its grip for minutes at a time as this thing did, or send me plunging through a ten foot high window to the ground below.

The first indication I had that these visitations were absolutely out of the ordinary course of events came on May 30th. About midnight I was suddenly awakened by a voice calling loudly, 'Look Out,' and at once I became aware of a red serpent coiling and uncoiling itself under my bed, and reaching out on to the floor with its head. Just as it was about to attack me I jumped through my window, and came to earth among the rose bushes below, fortunately with no more damage than a badly bruised arm.

After this there was absolute peace until June 30th, when the real climax came. I had seen the thing again on the night of the new moon, and had noticed considerable changes in its appearance. Especially it seemed far more active, while its long hair had changed into serpent-heads. The night after I was awakened by a violent noise and jumped out of bed. I then saw the noise was caused by a great red obelisk which crashed through the west wall of my room, and leaned against the wall at the east end, smashing both that and the window to pieces but missing my bed, which was in an alcove to the left of its path. In its transit it had smashed all the mirrors, and the floor and top of my bed were strewn with broken glass and fragments of wood. This time the obsession must have lasted some minutes. I dared not move for fear of cutting myself, and to reach the matches – wherein, I knew, lay safety – I had to lean across the bed and again risk the glass. Yet in my heart I knew that all this was false, but had no power to move. I could only stand there, incapable, looking at the shattered room in a state of hopeless terror.

And now comes the most extraordinary part of the whole business. When I had finally mastered the obsession, I went to bed again dead tired, and I know that the only sound I made that night was jumping to the floor, also my room is at least a hundred yards from the rest of my family, yet next morning at breakfast I was asked what was the terrible noise in my room during the night.

After that I realised that the game was up. I had not taken these occurrences lying down, but I knew that it was impossible for me to control the force which I had set in motion. In desperation I turned to a good friend, who, I was aware, knew much of these things. She did not hesitate, but came at once to my assistance, and from that day to the present the trouble has absolutely gone from me.

It seems likely that 'the good friend who knew much of these things' referred to by the anonymous author of the above account was Dion Fortune, a magician, medium and lay analyst – she trained at the Tavistock Clinic – who played such an important part in the occult world during the years 1922–45 that our next chapter is entirely devoted to her and the fraternity she founded.

Some alchemists, men and women who worked individually rather than in association, were also active in Britain during the interwar years. These, however, were exceptional. For in Britain, unlike France, the rebirth of magic has not been accompanied by any pronounced alchemical renaissance. Of the early members of the Golden Dawn only Ayton seems to have engaged in physical alchemy. Several members of the order were, however, students of a curious mesmeric interpretation of alchemy put forward *circa* 1850 by a Mrs. Attwood. This interpretation is difficult to understand; but it seems to affirm, firstly, that many alchemical works were disguised treatises on 'the higher phenomena of mesmerism', e.g. clairvoyance, and, secondly, the possibility of the achievement of a state of deep mesmeric trance in which the mind would be able, of itself, to transmute base metals into gold.

Westcott displayed a mild interest in alchemy and produced, *circa* 1890, a Flying Roll – a semi-official Golden Dawn manuscript – in which he expounded his views on the subject. These were not of any great profundity, although his attempts to classify such elements as Bromine and Chlorine in accordance with qabalistic symbolism are not without a quaint charm. He summed up his occult interpretation of alchemy in the final paragraphs of the Flying Roll:

> . . . I believe it is useless for anyone to waste time on purely chemical experiments. To perform alchemical processes requires a simultaneous operation on the astral plane with that on the physical. Unless you are Adept enough to act by willpower, as well as by heat and moisture, by life force as well as by electricity, there will be no adequate result.
>
> So far as I know . . . power of transmutation may arise side by side with other magical attainments. Work conquers all. It is not conferred by any grade. It is occasionally rediscovered by the private student. It is never actually taught in so many words. It may dawn on any one of you, or the magic event may occur when least expected.

In spite of Westcott's specific statement that no magical grade conferred the power of transmutation the Secret Chiefs supplied Mathers with detailed instructions as to how the Adepti Minores could carry out alchemical processes. These formed part of the manuscript Z2, the reception of which had so exhausted Mathers, and were an adaptation of the Golden Dawn neophyte ceremony; the substance to be transmuted being, so to speak, the candidate for initiation.

The alchemical processes outlined in Z2, denounced by Aleister Crowley as 'absolute rubbish' although he never seems to have made the slightest attempt to carry them out, are magical rather than chemical. They involve the adept in invoking Jupiter, Saturn and 'the head and tail of the dragon' and evoking an elemental to make an 'astral examination' of the material being worked upon. In spite of the very specific nature of the instructions not a single early Golden Dawn initiate ever seems to have attempted to apply them. In the 1960s, however, at least one occultist was using alchemical processes derived from Z2 in attempts to transform homoeopathic remedies into something approaching the legendary Elixir of Life.

A less ceremonial approach to the hermetic art has also had its English and Scottish devotees. One of the most interesting of these was Archibald Cockren (died *circa* 1950), a man who would seem to have succeeded in growing the mysterious 'alchemical tree'. This wonder was described by Paracelsus:

> It is possible also that Gold, through industry, and skill of an expert Alchymist may be so far exalted, that it may grow in a glasse like a tree, with many wonderfull boughs, and leaves, which indeed is pleasant to behold and most wonderfull. . . . thou seest the Gold to rise in the glasse, and grow after the manner of a tree . . . and so there is made of Gold a wonderfull and pleasant shrub, which the Alchymists call their Golden hearb, and the Philosophers Tree. . . .

The poet C.R. Cammell saw such a 'hearb' growing in Cockren's alchemical laboratory and observed it over a period of some months. At first it was very small, but eventually it grew considerably, the form of its leaves somewhat resembling those of a cactus. Other wonders which Cockren displayed were the 'Philosophers' Wine' and a 'potable elixir of gold'. Two phials of the last-mentioned substance were given to Mr. Cammell by the alchemist; the former described it as smelling and tasting like 'sweet flowers'. He found it an effective antidote, when taken in wine, to physical and nervous exhaustion, and recorded that, after taking it, he 'experienced little fatigue or nervous depression, required little sleep or food, and both felt and looked healthful and invigorated'.

The basis of this elixir was very probably what Cockren called 'the alkahest' – a substance he had prepared after many years of work, which had culminated as follows:

> The first intimation I had of this triumph was a violent hissing, jets of vapour pouring from the retort and into the receiver like sharp bursts from a machine-gun . . . whilst a very potent and subtle odour filled the laboratory and its surroundings . . . this odour . . . resembling the dewy earth on a June morning, with the hint of growing flowers in the air . . . and the sweet smell of the rain on the parched earth. . . .

Cockren has had many successors in recent years. One of the most surprising of them is Prince Stanislas Klossowski de Rolla – a man referred to by at least one gossip columnist as 'the playboy alchemist'. The Prince has been internationally known as one of 'the beautiful people' since the 1960s, when he was on friendly terms with the members of such rock groups as the Beatles and the Rolling Stones. At the time of writing his most recent newsworthy activity was his part in organising the fun and games at the weekend parties given by Victor Lownes, former chief of the British *Playboy* empire. His alchemical beliefs seem to be sincerely held and his essay on alchemy, published in Thames & Hudson's *Art and Imagination* series, makes curious and interesting reading.

In the USA alchemists are also active and the Paracelsus Research Society, already mentioned in relation to the New Zealand temple of the Stella Matutina, issues 'alchemical laboratory bulletins'. One well known American occultist has been sufficiently impressed by these and other practical instructions issued by the society to spend time in the preparation of a substance called 'the antimonial firestone'.

The *Alchemist's Handbook*, written by 'Frater Albertus', who would seem to be the presiding genius of the Paracelsus Research Society, is largely concerned with the production of herbal elixirs by alchemical means. It is clear, however, that Frater Albertus has carried out a great deal of experimentation on metals and minerals. For in an appendix to the *Handbook* he refers to such personal achievements as the preparation of vinegar of antimony 'according to the formula of Valentine' and the manufacture of the 'essences' of lead, copper, and gold.

The *Handbook*, which has also been published in German, has enjoyed a modest success, and an increasing number of American occultists are concerning themselves with alchemy. On the whole, however, it has been ceremonial magic which has attracted most Americans working within the western esoteric tradition. Such American magicians are dealt with in later chapters.

10 Dion Fortune and the Inner Light

Dion Fortune, magician, novelist and early follower of C.G. Jung, was born at the Welsh holiday resort of Llangollen in 1891. She was then named Violet Mary Firth – her pseudonym of Dion Fortune was not adopted until over thirty years later – and her parents, devout Christian Scientists, were the proprietors of a small hotel.

Violet was brought up in her parents' faith. She was taught that sickness, pain, and even death itself were illusions born of the sinfulness of what Mary Baker Eddy, founder of Christian Science, called 'mortal mind' and she was encouraged to recite 'there is no pain in truth therefore there is no truth in pain' and other extracts from *Science and Health*, the Christian Science textbook, to her parents' guests.

Violet was a precocious child and while still very young displayed a marked tendency to daydream and some talent for English composition. The former characteristic worried her parents but they encouraged her juvenile attempts at authorship and published, at their own expense, two small books of her essays, *Violets* and *More Violets*. Considering the age at which Violet wrote these essays they undeniably showed some literary promise, but their style is over-sweet by today's standards and some find them to possess distinctly emetic qualities.

A few years before World War I, when she was twenty years old, she underwent a traumatic experience from which it took her many years to recover. She was at the time 'living in' as a junior teacher in a boarding school and her employer was a domineering, extremely bad tempered woman who had lived in India for many years and had acquired some knowledge of oriental occultism. According to Violet this woman controlled her staff by a form of mind-power akin to hypnosis and, not surprisingly, there were a whole series of 'nervous breakdowns' among her staff. Eventually Violet antagonized this woman by foiling an attempt by her to gain control of the money of an elderly and rather simple-minded woman who was resident in the school. To avoid her employer's wrath she resigned her position, but before she was allowed to leave the establishment she was compelled to undergo a four hour long 'interview'. During this protracted and very unpleasant session her employer subjected her to a destructive form of hypnotic suggestion, repeating, time and time again, the phrases 'you are incompetent' and 'you have no self-control'. At first Violet refused to give way, but eventually some inner voice told her that her only hope of mental survival was to simulate a collapse of all resistance; she went down on her knees, swore never to leave her job and promised perpetual obedience. Then she returned to her room and lay on her bed in a semi-stupor for three days, showing all the symptoms of intense physical fear. A few days later her family came and took her home in a state of complete physical and emotional exhaustion. She herself compared the condition of her body to that of a discharged electric battery and claimed, in the terminology of occultism, that her etheric double was damaged and leaking *prana* (energy).

She did not completely recover from the effects of this distressing experience until almost ten years later when she was initiated into the Neophyte grade of the Golden Dawn. Within an hour of the ceremony, so she claimed, she felt herself healed.

The temple into which Dion Fortune had been admitted – from now on we shall call her by the name under which she wrote and which was an anglicized form of her magical motto – was what she described as 'the Southern branch of the Scottish section of the Order'. In other words, an English temple under the jurisdiction of J.W. Brodie-Innes. This temple was under the chieftainship of Maiya Curtis-Webb (later Mrs. Tranchell-Hayes), an occultist of real ability and great physical charm whose personality seems to have fascinated her young pupil; almost twenty years later she was to portray Maiya Curtis-Webb in fictionalised form as the ageless, enchanting heroine of her novels *Sea Priestess* and *Moon Magic*.

In spite of the high regard in which Dion Fortune held her chief, it was only a year or two after her initiation that she decided to transfer her allegiance to another temple under the control of a Mrs. Morgan-Boyd, the lieutenant and financial patron of Moina MacGregor Mathers herself. We are unaware of the exact reason for this change, but it is possible that she wanted to be nearer the centre of (magical) things, and that already she was beginning to display that lust for power which in later years was to become one of the more noticeable factors in the make-up of her complex personality.

Dion Fortune was extremely impressed with the teachings of the Golden Dawn. Here, she felt, was an occult method that really worked, here was the secret knowledge for which she had been unconsciously searching for many years. She was decidedly less impressed with her fellow-initiates, describing them as 'widows and grey-bearded ancients' and drily remarking of Mathers' widow that 'the mantle of Elijah had not descended on Mrs. Elisha'. Moina Mathers, on the other hand, was at first quite friendly towards her new recruit and the latter responded by making various suggestions designed to increase the membership of the Order.

There is little doubt that a few years earlier such suggestions would have been disregarded; while her husband was alive Moina Mathers had been quite as dedicated to secrecy and to keeping the Order small, select and of high quality as he himself. By this time, however, things had begun to change, Mrs. Mathers was hankering after an occult empire, and Dion Fortune's suggestions were met with enthusiasm. The latter's principal point was that Mathers' magical system was too intellectual and advanced for the ordinary student of occultism; what was needed, she urged, was a public society which could be used as a means of attracting suitable candidates into the Order. A sort of magically orientated Theosophical Society, holding lectures and issuing a magazine, but having no open connection with the Golden Dawn.

Thus, in 1922, the Fraternity of the Inner Light came into existence. For the first few years of its existence, however, it operated as The Christian Mystic Lodge of the Theosophical Society (President, Dion Fortune) – Dion Fortune had hoped to use the Theosophical Society as a sort of trawling-ground out of which suitable fish could be drawn into the nets of the Golden Dawn and it was not until 1928 that the Fraternity of the Inner Light came officially into existence and the *Christian Mystic*, supposedly a Theosophical journal, was overnight transformed into the *Inner Light Magazine*.

Long before this there had been a sharp deterioration in the friendly relationship between Dion Fortune and her supposed chief. It was not that Mrs. Mathers disapproved of the Christian Mystic Lodge and its willingness to sacrifice quality to quantity, for she herself had gone to even greater lengths, authorising the publication of an American pamphlet offering to confer initiation by post in return for a fee of ten dollars; it was rather that she had become aware that Dion Fortune, already engaging in astral travel and getting the supposed messages from 'the Masters' later published as *The Cosmic Doctrine*, was beginning to build up a little occult following of her own. Moina Mathers seems to have seen this as a potential threat to her own authority and looked about for an excuse to expel her former favourite from the Order. Her first attempt was unsuccessful; she suspended Dion Fortune for allegedly 'betraying the inner secrets of the Order' in her book *Esoteric Philosophy of Love and Marriage*, but she had to withdraw this suspension after it had been pointed out to her that Dion Fortune had not yet received the grade of the Order in which similar teachings were given. Later she again suspended Dion Fortune, this time for writing a series of articles for the *Occult Review* (later republished in book form as *Sane Occultism*), and finally expelled her after making the quite unanswerable accusation that certain symbols had not appeared in her aura.

In spite of her expulsion Dion Fortune persisted in using the Order system and set up a temple of her own in the Bayswater district of London. Officially this temple was affiliated to the Stella Matutina but in practice its chief went her own way, brooked no interference from anyone, and taught her pupils her own highly personal synthesis of magic and Jungian psychology instead of the Golden Dawn system in its entirety.

According to Dion Fortune's own account, Moina Mathers responded to this rebellion 'by resorting to black magic' and launching a 'psychic attack' upon her former subordinate. In her *Psychic Self Defence* (Rider, 1930), Dion Fortune told the story of this uncanny magical battle. She was afflicted with a plague of black and smelly tom-cats; worst of all she encountered an enormous tabby cat, twice the size of a tiger, strolling down her stairs. Dion Fortune exorcised her home, thus freeing herself of cats natural and supernatural, and eventually managed to overcome her opponent on the astral plane, although in the process she was, so she said, severely scratched 'because of the phenomena of repercussion'.

All this should not be taken too seriously. *Psychic Self Defence*, an occult best-seller, contains many stories of alleged psychic attacks, all of them probably greatly exaggerated, some of them almost certainly untrue. For example it tells the story of how its author succeeded in 'breaking the psychic link' between an obsessed woman and a sinister group of oriental occultists; all very exciting, no doubt, but the tale bears a remarkable resemblance to a personal experience of Dr. Berridge which he recounted in an early, semi-official, Golden Dawn side-lecture on the power of the imagination – a document with which Dion Fortune must have been familiar. Similarly, she recounted how she had accidentally created an artificial elemental by means of a partial astral projection. This entity, a were-wolf, almost got out of her control but, fortunately, after a prolonged struggle, she succeeded in re-absorbing it into her system! Once again a good, spine-chilling story – but clearly derived from an incident in Aleister Crowley's brilliant occult novel *Moonchild*, which was published at the very time when she was engaged in writing her own book.

In another section of *Psychic Self Defence* Dion Fortune went so far as to imply that Moina Mathers was guilty of the murder of a former associate of hers, a certain Miss Fornario, a student of occultism who had died in mysterious circumstances on the Scottish Isle of Iona. Certainly if there was such a murder it could only have been of an astral nature, for Moina Mathers died some months before Miss Fornario, a fact that Dion Fortune omitted to mention in her account of the tragedy.

Ten years after its birth the Fraternity of the Inner Light had been built up into an effective and tightly-knit occult order by its founder. She had by now grown very fat and had begun to bear some resemblance to an advertisement for Sandeman's Port, wearing a voluminous black coat and a floppy, wide-brimmed hat while taking her daily stroll through Hyde Park, but she still kept the growing membership of the Fraternity very much under her own surveillance. In her case obesity did not imply inactivity.

At this period in her life she entered into a correspondence with Aleister Crowley (whom she regarded with a mixture of repugnance for his character and admiration for his knowledge of the magical tradition), and visited him at least once. On that occasion she asked for his advice as to how she should conduct a planned invocation of the god Mercury. After a consultation with one of his disciples, a certain Frater V.I. who was supposedly an expert on the matter – some years before, while still at Oxford, he had invoked the god Thoth, an Egyptian form of Mercury, to visible appearance – Crowley urged her to stop all the clocks at her Fraternity headquarters and to go on a diet of steamed cod and sweet white wine. Frater V.I., anxious to see how far she would go, urged her to supplement this monotonous fare with a daily glass of fresh cockerel's blood taken at breakfast time. Frater V.I., who is still alive and no longer a Crowleyan, has assured one of us that Dion Fortune obeyed the advice to the letter. Unfortunately he was unable to say whether Mercury did or did not oblige with one of his rare personal appearances.

Many members of the Fraternity of the Inner Light had first become aware of its existence as a result of reading one or other of the many books written by Dion Fortune. Apart from her fiction most of these were no more than rather vulgar, pot-boiling occult journalism, but one of them, *The Mystical Qabalah*, first published in 1935, is considered by many occultists to be a classic of the occidental magical tradition. While the version of the qabalah expounded in this book bears no more than a marginal resemblance to the traditional mysticism of Israel, there is no doubt that Dion Fortune succeeded in conveying the main outlines of MacGregor Mathers' revised version of the Christian qabalism of the Renaissance in an easily comprehensible form. There are, however, one or two odd variations from the Golden Dawn qabalah. Some of these are very minor and probably resulted from hastiness in work and printers' errors not picked up in the proof-reading – for example, the Hebrew spelling is sometimes defective. Others are of real significance and would seem to indicate either that Dion Fortune had never completely mastered Golden Dawn qabalism or, perhaps more likely, that she had revised Mathers' system in accordance with teachings received from the astral Masters with whom she believed herself to be in communication.

Thus paragraph 13, Chapter XX of *The Mystical Qabalah* reads:

> When the glyph of the Fall [of Adam in the Garden of Eden] is represented on the Tree [of Life] it is interesting

to note that the heads of the Great Serpent that rises out of Chaos only come as far as Tiphareth [the solar centre on the Tree of Life] and do not overpass it.

To understand the significance of this passage it is essential to grasp the fact that the authentic Golden Dawn tradition attaches much importance to the doctrine of the Fall and believes it to express fundamental psychological and spiritual truths. It is not, of course, that Golden-Dawn-inspired occultists, past or present, believe in the literal truth of the story as told in *Genesis* – that the serpent entered the Garden in which God had placed the first humans, induced Eve to eat a forbidden fruit, and so on – but that they believe that the story allegorically presents the facts about some great spiritual disaster which has left mankind flawed and imperfect in a way in which other orders of being (such as cats, elephants and angels) are *not* flawed and imperfect. At some stage of evolution humanity has taken a wrong turning, it has developed in a way not in accordance with the Divine plan, and the souls of men – in their lower aspects at least – are grotesque perversions of what they were intended to be. This spiritual deformation has affected the material world; the horrors of Vorkuta, Auschwitz and 'Democratic Kampuchea' were some of the outward manifestations of the Fall.

This doctrine was expressed by Mathers and his associates in two 'altar diagrams' of the Garden of Eden, before and after the Fall, which were shown to Golden Dawn members in the course of the 'elemental' initiations. The first symbolised the archetypal man as he should be, and as he was before the prime deviation from the divine plan – a crowned figure, arms extended, the 'spheres' of the Tree of Life integrated with his body, and, imprisoned below his feet, the heads of the Serpent, representing the unbalanced and destructive forces of 'Chaos and Old Night'.

The second diagram, 'the Garden of Eden after the Fall', was a symbolic representation of the human spirit after the deviation; the Serpent had burst his restraining bonds and had raised his devouring heads up the kingly body so that they threatened the lowest seven of the ten 'spheres'. In other words, the Fall had deformed all but the three highest aspects of the human spirit; the physical body, the astral and mental 'bodies' had all been distorted, and thus diverted from conforming to the patterns appropriate to them.

Dion Fortune, in the brief extract we have reproduced above, was saying that the heads of the Serpent had 'only come as far as Tiphareth', i.e. that only five and not seven of the 'spheres' had been affected by the Fall, that mankind's deviation was not as great as the Golden Dawn had taught.

In spite of these and other variations from the Golden Dawn system *The Mystical Qabalah* is well worth reading and provides an excellent introduction to the subjects of which it treats. Much can also be learned from Dion Fortune's novels and short stories about what their author called 'the Western Esoteric Tradition' – in other words, the magic of Mathers and the Golden Dawn.

It is a curious fact that over the last eighty or so years there has been a considerable presentation of western occult teaching under the guise of fiction. Many of the authors who have produced this have not themselves been practising magicians, but their adoption of the conceptual framework of occultism has, nonetheless, enabled them to write works which painlessly convey occult theories to their readers. Thus, for example, Sax Rohmer presented the concept of ancient otherworldly forces, somehow locked outside the main stream of evolutionary development, in his entertaining *Brood of the Witch Queen*. Other supernatural fiction has been written by practising occultists in a deliberate attempt to convey what they held to be spiritual truths – we have already mentioned Lytton's *Zanoni*, Crowley's *Moonchild* and Brodie-Innes's *The Devil's Mistress*. Dion Fortune was perhaps the most successful of this school.

She began by writing short stories for the *Royal*

Magazine. These, later published in collected form as *The Secrets of Dr. Taverner* and still in print today, dealt with the adventures of an 'occult detective' of the type of Le Fanu's Martin Hesselius and Algernon Blackwood's John Silence. The experiences of this detective, as chronicled by his companion, a man almost as stupid as Holmes's Dr. Watson and Poirot's Captain Hastings, covered a wide field – vampirism, elemental spirits in human bodies, and the use of black magic to induce suicide, for example. The main fault of the stories is that the characters rarely come alive. The protagonist, Dr. Taverner, whom Dion Fortune said was a fictional representation of one of her own occult teachers, is a man of such intelligence, spiritual goodness, and magical power that it is difficult for the reader to achieve that 'willing suspension of disbelief' induced by such masters of the supernatural as Arthur Machen and M.R. James.

The first of Dion Fortune's novels, *Demon Lover*, was a fairly ordinary piece of horror, complete with adventures on the astral plane, vampirism and even a type of necromancy. The heroine was over-sweet, incredibly innocent, and remarkably virtuous. The two novels that succeeded this first effort were more successful; *Goatfoot God* told the story of a sexually repressed man who found relief through magic, marriage, and the recovery of his memory of a previous incarnation as an even more sexually repressed 16th century monk; *Winged Bull* was also concerned with sex, in this case with the magical *Mass of the Winged Bull* designed to unify the spiritual and physical aspects of male-female relationships. Her most successful novels from both the literary and occult points of view, were *Sea Priestess*, rejected by three different publishers and eventually printed at her own expense, and its posthumously published sequel, *Moon Magic*. In these two books she gave her own diagnosis of what she considered to be the spiritual sickness of modern man – he lacked, so she claimed, contact with the Black Isis, the primordial power-aspect of femininity – and her prescription for his recovery; this was to be achieved by a proper understanding of the magical doctrine of polarity. Every woman was to be a priestess of the Black Isis, every man was to understand her force and from the interplay of the male-female polarity was to be created a vortex which would bring down into manifestation the power of the primordial Isis, Mother of Gods and Men.

During World War II Dion Fortune returned to spiritualism, one of the interests of her earlier years, and enjoyed a successful career as a medium. Like other mediums she had her own 'guides' and she was a popular performer at spiritualist meetings, giving demonstrations of clairvoyance and trance mediumship.

Some years ago the occultist and writer Bernard Bromage, who knew Dion Fortune well at this period of her life, published in *Light* an amusing description of the headquarters of the Fraternity of the Inner Light at this late stage of its founder's career. According to this, beginners in the study of the occult arts and sciences were dealt with on the ground floor. Immediately above them rather more advanced souls were given what sounds suspiciously like a watered-down version of the Christian mysticism of the late mediaeval *devotio moderna*. At the top of the building, as near to heaven as possible, were the select few who studied the qabalah, practised magic, and were privileged to hear the teachings received by Dion Fortune from the Secret Chiefs, with whom she was in almost continuous communication. One of these was the Master R. – a superhuman being who will be encountered again in the next chapter – who seems to have been the source of much wisdom, including the revelation that the honey bee had originally been brought to this world from the planet Venus.

During the early years of the Fraternity of the Inner Light its initiation rituals would seem to have been only slightly modified versions of those used in the Golden Dawn – the 'Outer Greater Mysteries' ceremony, for example, being derived from Mathers' Portal rite. Amendments were introduced and, subsequently, major revisions. Eventually the Inner Light workings bore little or no resemblance to those from which they were descended.

Dion Fortune died in 1948. For some time the work of her foundation went on in very much the same way as it had done under her leadership. She had, however, been such a dominating personality, that it is not surprising that after a few years there was a notable reaction against her posthumous influence.

Initiates of her Fraternity began to study the works of Alice A. Bailey, huge volumes dictated to her by the Masters and conveying teachings which seem to be advanced developments of those of Madame Blavatsky. Some Inner Light members found these teachings stimulating and came to hold them in high regard. Others found them to have distinct soporific qualities.

Later on far more surprising sources exercised some influence on the Fraternity. Initiates were encouraged to change their postures and ways of movement in accordance with the Alexander technique, a system developed by a New Zealand singer, which had attracted some eminent devotees but was – and is – regarded with scepticism by both orthodox medicine and such fringe disciplines as osteopathy and chiropractice. This was harmless enough, but a significant minority of Inner Light members were irritated when they were urged to spend substantial sums of money in order to sit with E-meters – crude devices for measuring the electrical resistance of the skin – in their hands. This was a feature of 'processing', part of the dianetics and scientology invented by the science-fiction writer L. Ron Hubbard.

Dion Fortune's grade structure also came under attack because elements of 'glamour' – that is, illusion – were discerned in it, probably rightly. At about the same time the type of mediumship by which the Fraternity's founder had usually contacted the Secret Chiefs was abandoned in favour of a new process, alleged to be much superior, called 'mediation'. The teachings received by this mediation were conveyed to the membership through a series of 'A.F. Papers'. The contents of these are, of course, copyright and, in any case, the precise nature of the teachings given in them does not concern anyone save members of the Fraternity. It suffices to say that those who read them can, broadly speaking, be divided into two groups. The first finds both the teachings and the style in which they are expressed repellent, reminiscent of Catholic pietism at its very worst. The second finds them of real importance, perhaps sugary in tone, but expressing profound spiritual truths.

While not a secret society, in the sense of the Chinese Tongs and brotherhoods of the sort founded by Michael Bakunin, the Inner Light is, like the freemasons, 'a society with secrets'. Thus outsiders such as ourselves can have no detailed knowledge of what has gone on inside it in recent years. There is some reason to believe, however, that in this period there has been 'a reaction against the reaction' and that today Dion Fortune and her writings are more esteemed within the Inner Light than they were twenty years ago.

A certain number of those who left the Society at one stage or another of its life have also done much to keep Dion Fortune's teachings alive. Such have either founded occult groups – at least one of these uses the old Inner Light rituals – while others have become independent occult teachers and/or writers.

One of the most notable of these is 'Gareth Knight', a writer whose Arthurian pseudonym reflects a strong interest in the Holy Grail and 'the Matter of Britain'. This interest was probably derived from Dion Fortune, whose attitude towards Camelot and the doings of its knights was such that she instructed her pupils to study and meditate upon Malory's *Morte d'Arthur*. Mr. Knight's first book, a two volume study of qabalistic symbolism, is an excellent guide to the Golden Dawn – Mathers – Fortune version of the qabalah, although, in the opinion of some, it is marred by some elements derived from the post-Dion-Fortune Inner Light – for example, an enthusiastic reference to scientological processing. His later books make better reading.

A writer who has expressed the occult teachings of Dion Fortune as reflected in an Anglican mirror is the Rev. Anthony Duncan, a priest whose *Lord of the Dance* (Helios, 1972) is well worth reading.

Almost all of Dion Fortune's books, save for an enthusiastic study of the soya bean as an article of diet, have remained continuously in print throughout the last twenty years. They have proved a major influence on the rebirth of magic. It seems certain that they will continue to exert such an influence for many years to come.

11 Ritual Magic in the United States

S A M H A I N

F E S T I V A L

Sun., Oct. 26, 1–6 p.m.

at

INFERNO DISCO

5 West 19th Street
New York

Tickets $6 in advance . . . Bar will be open for drinks. No controlled substances please!

BANDS . . . Master of Ceremonies – 'Simon'

Ishtar dancing the Dance of the Seven Veils
Convocation by Dr. Leo Louis Martello
Samhain Ritual by Earthstar Coven
Thelemic Ritual by Lashtal Lodge, O.T.O.

So, in part, reads a leaflet issued in the fall of 1980 to advertise New York's '5th Annual Pagan Samhain[1] Festival'. The regular annual celebration of this feast, with rituals conducted by both disciples of Aleister Crowley and devotees of modern witchcraft, is symptomatic of the current importance of the USA as *the* centre of the revival of western magic and alchemy. And yet it is only in the last sixty years or so that esoteric cults of European derivation have begun to play any considerable part in American occultism.

It is true, of course, that in the 17th and 18th centuries there had been one or two American alchemists – notably a certain Dr. Child, one of the political group known as the Remonstrants – and that Cotton Mather and other New England clerics had shown a marked interest in magic, witchcraft and ghosts; but at the time when English occultists were studying the writings of Lévi and Francis Barrett their American opposite numbers were confining their attentions to mesmerism, the phenomena of spiritualism, and the oriental occultism of Madame Blavatsky's Theosophical Society. Even P.B. Randolph, a mulatto who set up an allegedly Rosicrucian Society and attempted to expand his consciousness by the use of ether and other psychedelic substances, seems to have left ritual magic severely alone.

The first serious American student of Lévi was a masonic dignitary named Albert Pike – he was Grand Commander of the *Southern Jurisdiction of the Ancient and Accepted Rite of Freemasonry*. In 1871 he published his *Morals and Dogma*, over 850 closely printed pages of qabalistic, masonic, and occult exposition. In his preface to this volume, weighty in every sense of the word, Pike explained that only half of it was his own work; the remainder, he explained, he had extracted from 'the works of the best writers and most philosophic or eloquent thinkers.' Most of these extracts (reproduced by Pike without quotation marks) came from the writings of Lévi, particularly from the *Dogma and Ritual* and the *History of Magic*.

Whether or not Albert Pike actually practised ceremonial magic, as distinct from reading and theorizing about it, is uncertain, but there is no doubt that his opponents regarded him as a magician of the darkest hue, a veritable worshipper of Satan. Most of these antagonists belonged to the Catholic Church and it must be admitted that they had some reason to dislike Pike, for the latter regarded the Church with such a deep loathing that he was obsessed not only by such comparatively recent events as the ecclesiastical condemnation of Galileo but by the 14th century suppression of the Knights Templar! He wrote that 'from the tomb in which after his murders he rotted Clement the Fifth howls against the successors of his victims . . . the ghosts of the dead Templars haunt the Vatican and disturb the slumbers of the paralysed Papacy which, dreading the dead, shrieks out its excommunications and impotent anathemas against the living . . .'

If this language was extreme, so was that in which the lunatic fringe of extreme Catholicism denounced Pike and his allegedly diabolical magical activities. Thus in *The Devil in the 19th Century* (Paris, 1893), a freemason named Walder is reported as saying that:

> At Charleston, every Friday afternoon at three o'clock we come face-to-face and are in direct communication with the Good God (i.e. the Devil). He is there before us, we see him and touch him, we humbly kiss his Divine hands. He speaks to us. Our Sovereign Pontiff, that most holy and sublime brother Albert Pike, never writes one of his encyclicals until the most essential passages have been dictated to him. The Holy of Holies . . . has been placed in our care and nobody can enter it save for the Sovereign Pontiff and the ten members of the Supreme College, who in it are regularly visited by Lucifer-God, our omnipotent Lord.

If *Morals and Dogma* can be regarded as an encyclical, and we see no reason why it should not, it is to be presumed that its real author was Satan himself – always providing of course, that one can accept the veracity of Walder's statement. As, however, the author of *The Devil in the 19th Century* also claimed that he had been present at a Black Mass at which the officiating priest had washed his hands in molten lead, that he had visited underground workshops burrowed beneath Gibraltar where diabolists in the pay of the British Empire combined the worship of

Satan with the manufacture of poisons designed to be used against good Catholics; and that he had reliable evidence that Queen Victoria indulged in phallic orgies of the utmost depravity, it can safely be assumed that, whether or not Pike was a practising magician, he wrote his own books.

Another American student of Lévi was Emma Hardinge-Britten, a professional spiritualist medium who produced two books, *Ghostland* and *Art Magic*, largely derived from the writings of the French mage. She had been born an Englishwoman and had pursued an unsuccessful stage career before abandoning it in favour of trance mediumship; one observer of the latter remarked that he was inclined to accept its genuineness as he could not believe that her acting had so much improved. *Ghostland*, which its real author fathered on to a quite imaginary occultist named the Chevalier de B., originally appeared in 1872 as a serial in the *Western Star* of Boston. Its successor, subtitled *Mundane, Sub-Mundane and Super-Mundane Spiritualism*, was published two years later by subscription in an edition of 500 copies. It was divided into three parts. Both the first part, which dealt with the qabalah, and second, which dealt with the development of magic in the orient, were grossly inaccurate and stolen from Lévi. The final part of the book, which dealt with the actual techniques of evocation and invocation, was also stolen, this time from the Fourth Book of the *Occult Philosophy* of Agrippa, from the third edition of Scot's *Discoverie of Witchcraft*, and from the *Key of Solomon*. In spite of all this plagiarism *Art Magic* enjoyed some small success, for Americans with an inclination to occultism were beginning to become more interested in traditional magical technique and there was a dearth of printed material on the subject. It would seem that quite a few would-be magicians used *Art Magic* as a textbook and there is an occult rumour that as late as 1925 a group of cultists in Detroit were using rituals extracted from it as a means of 'controlling demons'.

By this time, however, better editions of the grimoires

and other magical textbooks had been made available to American readers by L.W. de Lawrence, a prolific pirate-publisher whose arrogance and conceit were surpassed only by his impertinence. He pirated A.E. Waite's *Pictorial Key to the Tarot* and claimed that he had written it himself; he produced a new edition of Francis Barrett's *The Magus* (originally published in 1801) under the ridiculous title of *Hindu Magic* and with his own name on the title page; and, with an effrontery that almost commands respect, he pirated Crowley's edition of the *Goetia of Solomon the King* and placed the words *Only Authorized Edition* on its front page. Apart from this he operated a mail-order business in occult charms and talismans, most of them derived from the degenerate Faust-books of 17th century Germany.

As has been noted earlier, the Golden Dawn had spread to the United States before the revolt of 1900 and a Thoth-Hermes Temple had been established in Chicago. Later on, in about 1912 or 1913, Mathers had conferred a number of ridiculously high grades on some Americans resident in Paris; in his *Equinox* Crowley claimed that one American woman, nominally an Exempt Adept, had paid Mathers hundreds of dollars for her high-sounding magical dignity. Some of these Parisian Americans seem to have been connected with the Societas Rosicruciana in America and in the twenties and thirties this organisation became the main source of a Mather-derived influence on American occultism.

The Societas Rosicruciana in America was the fourth attempt to establish an independent North American Rosicrucian jurisdiction: the first had been founded by Johann Kelpius in 1694[2], and had died out early in the 18th century; the second had been that of P.B. Randolph who, in 1858, had founded the Temple of the Rosy Cross; and the third had been the masonic Societas Rosicruciana in USA which had been established in 1878 and still survives as what may be regarded as a group of masonic antiquarians. The fourth foundation, the Societas Rosicruciana in America, was much more successful than its predecessors. It had originally been chartered in 1912 by its English opposite number and there is no doubt that the English masonic Rosicrucians who were responsible for its birth assumed that its membership would be confined, like that of their own society, to high-grade (and inevitably male) freemasons. Similarly they had taken it for granted that it would a) function as a secret society and b) make no public declaration of its allegiance to occultism and ritual magic. On the contrary, the American Rosicrucians opened their society to female membership, advertised correspondence courses in occultism and publicised a somewhat watered-down version of the magic of the Golden Dawn.

The main driving force of the SRIA was its Supreme Magus, a journalist named George Winslow Plummer. Plummer, born at Boston in 1876, had been ordained as a Roman Catholic priest but had rapidly grown tired of the Church, although not perhaps as tired as the Church had grown of him. Later on in life he had become a leading member of the American Birth Control League – he was a friend of Margaret Sanger, contraception's leading propagandist – and the presiding Archbishop of no less than three independent Churches!

The first of these ecclesiastical bodies was the Anglican Universal Church, the second was the Ecclesiae Rosicruciana Catholicae (otherwise known as the First Rosicrucian Church of America) which claimed, in Plummer's own words, 'to minister the major and minor sacraments and hold the Apostolic Orders and the Historic Episcopate'. Exactly how it could have acquired the 'Historic Episcopate' is uncertain, for while its priests claimed to have been ordained by a Puerto Rican named Manuel Ferrando, there is no evidence at all that Ferrando had ever been validly consecrated as a bishop. Plummer was on better ground with his third Archbishopric, that of the impressively titled *Holy Orthodox Church in America*, for he had been consecrated to this office by W.A. Nichols, himself consecrated by a quite genuine, although schismatic, Russian Orthodox bishop named Aftimios

Ofiesh. Plummer had probably met Nichols as a fellow journalist – the latter was religious editor of the *New York Telegram* and in 1934, the year he consecrated Plummer, he was, as one who knew him then was later to write, 'a sporty old dog. He wore his clericals in the newspaper office in New York. . . . He had a dollar up on the horses every afternoon. . . .'

Under Plummer the structure of the Rosicrucians was divided into three separate parts. The first of these was religious; apart from the previously mentioned Rosicrucian Church there was its associated Seminary for Biblical Research which gave correspondence courses in 'Christian Mysticism and Hermeneutics' – with, of course, a magical slant. The second section of the organisation included the American College of Astro-science, which ran correspondence courses in astrology, and other alleged seminaries and colleges which gave instruction in 'the spiritual aspects of Anthropology, Ethnology and Biology' – whatever they may have been. The third and most important Rosicrucian section dealt with occultism and magic; those who wanted to participate in its activities began by taking a correspondence course in Rosicrucian Principles (the prospectus for this course assured 'right-thinking men and women' that it would provide them with a 'veritable treasure-chest of spiritual principles'), went on to study something called 'the Secret Work of Spiritual Alchemy', and finally took the nine ritually conferred magical grades from Zelator to Prince Chief Adept. While the American Rosicrucians claimed that the rituals used for conferring these grades were the so-called Eckharthausen Ceremonies (i.e. the rituals of the 1777 reformation of German Rosicrucianism), surviving documents show that they were the rituals of the English masonic Rosicrucians heavily modified in accordance with the teachings of the Golden Dawn. The Society still survives at the present day and publishes a magazine called *Mercury*.

Enjoying a friendly relationship and a certain amount of cross-membership with the Societas Rosicruciana in

America were Golden Dawn temples that functioned more directly under the control of MacGregor Mathers and, later, his widow. These, like their European counterparts, suffered a series of splits, disagreements and magical battles, the exact history of which is almost impossible to follow. As a result of these there was a mushrooming of schismatic magical fraternities. Some of them kept fairly faithfully to the original Mathers system, others abandoned large parts of it and, like the Stella Matutina, became addicted to astral travel, and still others incorporated pieces from other occult systems (from, for example, the Esoteric Christianity of Max Heindel) into their teachings.

The most important and influential of these derivative groups was founded by the dedicated occultist Paul Foster Case.

Case, born in 1884, was a precocious child, reading almost before he could walk, beginning to play the piano at the age of three, and becoming the organist of a Congregational Church in Fairport, New York, only six years later.

Music was to remain an abiding passion, and at one time he seriously considered devoting his entire life to it. The lure of western occultism, which he had discovered as an adolescent, was, however, to prove stronger. He became fascinated by the tarot, which he studied intensely, and in time began, so he claimed, to hear an inner voice guiding him in his researches. There is no real reason to doubt this; as a child he could consciously manipulate his dream states and this ability – much sought after by western magicians as a means of controlling the astral world's 'Treasure House of Images' – is often associated with clairaudience, the hearing of other-worldly voices. Whether such voices emanate from non-human entities, good or evil, or whether they arise from the depths of the personal or collective unconscious, is, of course, a subject for dispute.

Case had no doubts. He believed that the voice he mentally heard was that of 'the Master R.' – one of those superbeings whom Mathers called 'The Secret Chiefs'.

The 'Master R.' (that is the 'Master Rakoczi'), also known as the Hungarian Master and usually identified with the 18th century alchemist and adventurer who called himself the Comte de Saint-Germain, had for more than a century been the subject of the adulation of those who believe in Masters and Secret Chiefs. Madame Blavatsky wrote that he 'was certainly the greatest Oriental Adept Europe has seen during the last centuries'; Isabel Cooper-Oakley, who wrote extensively on his life and adventures, described him as a messenger 'from the spiritual Hierarchy by whom the world's spiritual evolution is guided'; and Annie Besant, who claimed to have met him in the flesh on many occasions, the first being in 1896 at 19 Avenue Road, West London, asserted that he was 'still living in the same body the perennial youth of which astonished the observers of the 18th century'. A close associate of Annie Besant, a man who also claimed to have met Rakoczi in person, gave in 1911 a detailed outline based on 'astral and spiritual clairvoyance', of the activities, previous incarnations and interests of the Hungarian Master:

> The Head of the Seventh Ray is the Master the Comte de St. Germain, known to history in the eighteenth century, whom we sometimes call the Master Rakoczi, as He is the last survivor of that royal house. He was Francis Bacon, Lord Verulam, in the seventeenth century, Robertus the Monk in the sixteenth, Hunyadi Janos in the fifteenth, Christian Rosencreutz in the fourteenth, and Roger Bacon in the thirteenth, and He is the Hungarian Adept of A.P. Sinnett's book *The Occult World*. Further back in time he was Proclus, the great Neoplatonic philosopher, and before that St. Alban. He works to a large extent through ceremonial magic, and employs the services of great Angels, who obey Him implicitly and love to do His will. Though He speaks all European and many Oriental languages, much of His work is in Latin, the language which is the especial vehicle for His thought, and the splendour and

rhythm of it is unsurpassed by anything that we know down here. In His various rituals He wears wonderful and many-coloured robes and jewels. He has a suit of golden chain-mail, which once belonged to a Roman Emperor; over it is thrown a magnificent cloak of crimson, with on its clasp a seven-pointed star in diamond and amethyst, and sometimes He wears a glorious robe of violet. Though He is thus engaged with ceremonial, and still works some of the rituals of the Ancient Mysteries, even the names of which have long been forgotten in the outer world, He is also much concerned with the political situation in Europe, and the growth of modern physical science.

In Chicago, at some time before World War I, Case made contact with a man whom he believed to be an emissary from the Master. This emissary, who seemed to have a detailed knowledge of both Case's personal affairs and his innermost thoughts and desires, told him that he was at the great crossroads of his life. 'If,' he said, 'you decide to continue in your musical career you will be successful. You will have a little more of this world's goods than most. You will have a relatively happy and easy incarnation. However, if you take the other road, you will be dedicating yourself fully to serve humanity and play a vital part in its evolution for this coming Aquarian Age. Your life will be hard. You will be subjected to forces difficult to withstand. Tests and trials will be with you throughout your incarnation. Sorrow will walk with you often. You will not receive any recognition or glory. The recognition of your contribution to the evolution of humanity will start to come only after you have left your physical body. The Masters await your decision, for it will take them many earth years to find a suitable vehicle for the Vast Soul who will incarnate for the purpose of continuing the great work which you will have started in its revised phases for this era. The Masters promise nothing save to give help in all phases of the spiritual teachings. They wish you to know that hard though your life will be, in the final analysis you will not starve to death.'

Case decided to follow the 'tests and trials' of the western occultism of Mathers and Michael Whitty ('Frater Perseverantia'), his most devoted American follower. He was initiated into the Chicago 'Thoth-Hermes Temple' of the Golden Dawn, rose rapidly through the ritually conferred magical grades, and eventually became the 'Greatly Honoured Praemonstrator General' of this section of the order. At about the same time he began to contribute articles to H.W. Percival's magazine *The World*.

At this stage of events the Master R. once more intervened in Case's life. His manifestation which took place in New York, was physical but unalarming. He did not astonish the inhabitants of Manhattan by appearing clad in his golden chain-mail and crimson cloak. He did not even suddenly materialise to cause that dizziness and bleeding at the nose which Mathers found so exhausting a complement to the appearance of the Secret Chiefs and the transmission of their esoteric teachings to him. Instead he used the prosaic medium of the telephone, calling Case – who recognised the voice as identical to that which he had heard clairaudiently for many years – in order to inform him that he, the Master, was making a personal visit to the USA in order to supervise the preparation of his pupil for the task of beginning 'the next incarnation of the Qabalistic Way of Return'. This 'Way of Return' is, we suppose, the old Gnostic evolutionary process by which mankind is believed to be able to return to its divine source.

In other words the Master R. was telling Dr. Case – he had, it would seem, acquired a Doctorate in Theology from some source or another – that the Golden Dawn was finished as a vehicle for individual or collective spiritual advancement and that it was his job, with the aid of the Masters, to build a more satisfactory one.

There followed three weeks of intense personal instruction from the Master, at the end of which Dr. Case founded the Shrine of Ageless Wisdom, an esoteric school which later changed its name to The Builders of the

Adytum – the Adytum was the holy of holies in a classical temple – more usually known as B.O.T.A.

Case died in 1954, and was succeeded as the head of B.O.T.A. by Dr. Ann Davies, a lady who had been for some time, so she believed, receiving spiritual teaching from the same Master as Dr. Case. She died in 1975.

B.O.T.A. continues to flourish, offering correspondence courses in such subjects as occult psychology, the tarot and qabalah, spiritual alchemy, and various forms of healing involving the use of colour and sound. Those who successfully complete such courses may be admitted into a Pronaos – a local group affiliated to B.O.T.A. – where they may participate in ritual workings and, in time, officiate at the performance of such rituals.

Paul Foster Case's foundation is perhaps, the most impressive of the western, magically-orientated fraternities which openly and publicly seek new members.

Disciples of Aleister Crowley's Magick have been active in the USA from 1916 until the present. Some description of the more prominent of these, together with an account of the 'explosion' of American ritual magic that has taken place in the last twenty five years, is given in later chapters.

12 Sex Magic

The association of sex and religion, the idea that the orgasm can be applied to magical and mystical purposes, seems strange and perverted to most westerners – almost as perverted as Christianity's use of wine in one of its two major sacraments seems to the pious Muslim or Hindu.

Yet the concept is widespread in both India and China and, even in Europe, signs of occult sexual teachings and practices can be traced through the centuries.

Thus in 1411 a group of French heretics were accused of holding the belief that 'the natural sexual act could be performed in such a manner that it could be likened to an act of prayer'. A century later Cornelius Agrippa described copulation as 'full of magical endowment' and, not long afterwards, the mystic Aratus wrote that:

> As the physical union of male and female leads to the fruit from the composition of each, so the interior and secret association of male and female, is the copulation of the male and female soul, and is appointed for the production of fitting fruit of the divine life.

Thomas Vaughan, the 17th century alchemist, Rosicrucian and writer on magic, hinted at mystic aspects of sexuality:

> . . . life itself is nothing but a union of male and female principles, and he that perfectly knows this secret knows . . . how he ought to use a wife . . .

Sexual symbolism was in common use amongst alchemists and some of these undoubtedly adopted a literal interpretation of such alchemical phrases as 'the wedding of the King and Queen'. Even the grosser aspects of copulation were of interest to some alchemists, and a German account, based on 18th century records and quoted by Christopher McIntosh in his study of Rosicrucianism, gives details of a group which sought to find the secrets of transmutation by working upon sweat, semen and other bodily secretions. One of the members of the group was an officer in the Austrian army; he paid men under his command to supply him with semen obtained by means of masturbation. The affair was discovered – so goes the story – when the regimental surgeon was called in to treat the soldiers who had reduced themselves to weakness by the intensity of their autosexual activity. This alleged discovery throws some doubt upon the entire story. A healthy man ceases to be able to get erections, let alone ejaculations, long before hectic sexual activity can have any effect upon his physical health.

The first western occultists who openly advocated sexual magic and mysticism were P.B. Randolph, the American 'Rosicrucian' mentioned in the last chapter, and Thomas Lake Harris, the mystagogue of whom Dr. Berridge of the Golden Dawn was such a fervent disciple.

Randolph's system was based on the idea that during coition male and female psychic and physical secretions synthesise into a new and higher unity. The 'current' thus formed must 'flow' properly if both male and female are to achieve spiritual, mental, and physical well-being. Randolph taught his disciples how to create and manage this current of what he sometimes called 'nerve-aura'.

He claimed to have aquired his techniques in the Middle East:

> One night . . . I made love to, and was loved by, a dusky maiden of Arabic blood. I . . . learned . . . the fundamental principle of the White Magic of Love; subsequently I became affiliated with some dervishes and fakirs of whom . . . I found the road to other knowledges; and of these devout practisers of a simple, but

> sublime and holy magic, I obtained additional 'clues' – little threads of suggestion, which, . . . led my soul into labyrinths of knowledge. . . . I became . . . a mystic . . . actually discovering the ELIXIR OF LIFE; the universal solvent, or celestial alkahest; the water of beauty and perpetual youth, and the philosophers' stone . . .

Thomas Lake Harris invented – or perhaps rediscovered – a breathing technique which he called 'archnatural respiration' and may well have practised a sexual technique which involved a copulating couple breathing together in unison. Certainly Harris's disciple Laurence Oliphant taught just such a sexual-pneumatic method, which he called sympneumata. An adaptation of sympneumata has been widely used by modern sorcerers to achieve sexual conquests. This involves the would-be occult seducer breathing in exact unison with his intended victim for three to five minutes and then powerfully contracting the muscles of his rectum for a few seconds. This supposedly brings into action a psychic centre called the muladhara chakra and astrally links the two people involved. The man then increases his rate of breathing and concentrates his imagination on the sexual organs of the woman. This is believed to induce intense sexual arousal in the victim.

The first western occult fraternity to openly advocate and teach sexual magic was the Ordo Templi Orientis – the Order of Eastern Templars – usually known as the OTO.

The OTO originated in Germany, somewhere about the year 1906, as a result of the activities of Theodor Reuss, an occultist connected – as Mr. Ellic Howe has shown – with a large number of spurious and clandestine quasi-masonic lodges. Under the leadership of Reuss the OTO was surprisingly frank about the nature of its teachings. In an article published in 1912 Reuss claimed that:

> Our Order possesses the KEY which opens up all Masonic and Hermetic secrets, namely, the teaching of sexual magic, and this teaching explains, without excep-

tion, all the secrets of Nature, all the symbolism of Freemasonry and all systems of religion.

The German OTO was organised in nine grades. The first three bore a notable resemblance to the orthodox masonic grades of, respectively, Entered Apprentice, Fellow Craft and Master Mason. The next three grades were pseudomasonic – one of them, for example, was a parody of the Holy Royal Arch. Only the last three were, strictly speaking, concerned with sex magic. In the seventh degree some theoretical teachings were given to the initiate. In the eighth degree he was taught a sort of magical masturbation, being instructed to visualise a god or goddess as his sexual partner. He would be told to choose a particular deity for the purpose in accordance with whatever magical object he had in mind. If, for example, he wanted to achieve wisdom he would take Athene as his imaginary partner.

In the ninth grade the OTO initiate was taught an extension of this technique which used the method in association with heterosexual activity. This usually involved the sex magician in what was sometimes blasphemously referred to as 'taking the sacrament' – i.e. the consumption of some part of the mingled secretions of the male and female participants in the rite.

Under Reuss the OTO spread into several countries. The extraordinary thing, however, is that almost no member of the 'Reussian' OTO seems to have *practised* sex magic as distinct from talking and writing about it. Even Reuss himself is only on one occasion reported to have taken part in sexo-magical activities.

This situation was transformed in 1912, when Aleister Crowley was initiated into the OTO and given the splendid (but meaningless) title of 'Supreme and Holy King of Ireland, Iona and all the Britains (*sic*) Within the Sanctuary of the Gnosis'.

A British section of the OTO was established under the nominal leadership of Leila Bathurst, a mistress of Crowley, and acquired a modest following, most of whom were probably unaware of the eccentric sexo-magical techniques taught in the higher grades. It is unlikely, for example, that Dr. Felkin, the chief of the Stella Matutina, regarded the OTO, which he joined in 1913, as anything more than another masonic association.

Crowley was very impressed with Reuss's sexual teachings, incorporating them into his Magick and writing a number of short treatises upon them. These were intended for manuscript circulation to initiates of the higher grades of the OTO.

In all these, and most particularly in the tractates *Liber Agapé* and *De Arte Magica*, Crowley revealed in only slightly veiled forms the techniques of the OTO; as well as didactic matter derived from Reuss these works also contain some short chapters in which Crowley outlined his own sexual interpretations of such occult matters as blood sacrifice and vampirism. The latter he associated – anticipating the conclusions of several Freudians – with oral sex:

> The Vampire . . . exhausts the quarry by a suitable use of the body, most usually the mouth, without himself entering in any other way into the matter. And this is thought by some to partake of the nature of Black Magic. The exhaustion should be complete; if the work be skilfully executed, a few minutes should suffice to produce a state resembling, and not far removed from, coma. Experts may push this practice to the point of the death of the victim, thus obtaining not merely the physical strength, but imprisoning and enslaving the soul. This soul then serves as a familiar spirit.

It seems likely that Crowley and Reuss would have fallen out over which of them was to direct the OTO if communications between the two magicians had not been interrupted by the outbreak of World War I.

Reuss spent the years of 1915–21 in Switzerland. Allegedly he earned his living as a freelance journalist. More probably he was a German spy – he had worked for the Prussian political police in the 1880s and had been involved in German counter-intelligence activities soon after the outbreak of the war. His magical and political activities were curiously mingled at this period of his life. Thus in 1917 he organised an 'Anti-Nationalist Co-operative Congress', probably on the instructions of his military superiors, for, while the supposed aim of the conference was the encouragement of international brotherhood, its real purpose was the conversion of 'poisonous anti-German sentiments into something more fair to Germany'. In spite of the essentially political nature of this quite successful congress it was accompanied by the foundation of a new OTO lodge into which delegates were initiated – Reuss smilingly pocketing the fees – and certain activities discreetly described as 'orgiastic'.

In 1918 Reuss published a German version of the Gnostic Mass (see Chapter One) and, in spite of a stroke, continued his activities until his death in 1923.

After this the German OTO lodges were in continued disarray until, after the Nazi rise to power, they were compulsorily dissolved. For a short period in 1925 there was a temporary unity with Crowley recognised as 'Outer Head of the Order'; this ended in much quarrelling and the establishment of a number of associations claiming an OTO derivation.

The most interesting of these was Saturn-Gnosis, led by a magician who called himself Gregor A. Gregorius. This group taught a number of eccentric sexo-magical practices. Thus, for example, initiates were instructed to vary the positions they adopted during sexual intercourse in accordance with the angular relationships of the planets with the sun and moon.

With the Nazi suppression of occult associations the only active OTO magicians in the world – apart from Crowley and a few isolated individuals – were to be found in Canada and the United States.

Crowley had gone to the USA in the autumn of 1914 and spent most of the next six years in that country. He worked hard to establish the OTO in America but without much success, although small lodges and chapters of the order were established here and there. On one occultist who later became well-known he did exert some slight influence. The man in question was H. Spencer Lewis, the founder of AMORC ('Ancient and Mystical Order Rosae Crucis'), a popular and widely advertised esoteric fraternity whose publicity material has appeared in pulp magazines since the 1920s.

Lewis was altogether too slippery a fish to be caught in Crowley's net – he wanted to found an occult empire, not to be the subject of one – but he did come into contact with the 'Crowleyan' OTO and included some material drawn from that source in early versions of AMORC correspondence courses. We understand that he later amended or withdrew this material. It is significant, however, that in 1921 he obtained a charter from Reuss and that as late as 1929 he was in friendly correspondence with 'Frater Recnartus', then head of the German OTO and at one time an associate of Crowley. It is only fair to say that by this time Crowley and 'Recnartus' were on extremely unfriendly terms as the result of a visit the former had paid the latter. Crowley had been entertained so badly that he felt in real danger of death by starvation and had retaliated by putting an evil spell on the German magician's favourite cockerel . . .

After Crowley's departure from the USA he left the American OTO under the control of C.S. Jones, a man for whose magical expertise he had developed much respect. As time passed Jones became exceedingly odd in both his opinions and his behaviour. He decided, for example, that almost all the symbolism used by Crowley, a symbolism taken over lock-stock-and-barrel from the Golden Dawn, was muddled, and sorted it out to his own satisfaction by interpreting all qabalistic diagrams on the principle that they had mistakenly been drawn upside down. Some time later he decided that his occult knowledge was so vast that for him 'all veils were open'. To make this clear to all he took to walking the streets wearing nothing but a raincoat, now and then opening it wide to display his magical abilities to surprised pedestrians.

A spell in hospital followed, but Jones continued to run some sort of occult fraternity for the next twenty years or so. For a time the OTO was dormant, although it still nominally existed under the leadership of W.T. Smith.

The next serious attempt to establish OTO-derived sexual magic in the USA was made by C.F. Russell, a young occultist who had for a time been an inmate of the 'Abbey of Thelema' run by Crowley in Sicily during the early 1920s. The 'Abbey', a somewhat dilapidated farm-house, had been the scene of much magic, sexual and otherwise. It closed after a series of journalistic 'exposures', largely lies and half-truths, had appeared in the London *Sunday Express* and been picked up by the Hearst press. The latter gave Crowley's alleged murder of a young magician (of which he was totally innocent) much libellous coverage.

Russell's fraternity, originally called the Choronzon Club but later changing its name to the GBG – according to one source this stood for 'Great Brotherhood of God', which sounds unlikely – was first brought to the attention of American occultists by a series of advertisements in the *Occult Digest*. The advertisement, first appearing in 1931, promised:

A SHORT-CUT TO INITIATION

THE CHORONZON CLUB

Box 123, Chicago, Illinois

Like most other people, aspirants to initiation are attracted to short-cuts, and within a short time Russell had a larger American following than was ever achieved by Crowley himself. They were taught a simplified, and to some extent inverted, version of the magic of the Golden Dawn and the OTO. Thus Russell's pupils were taught to use the same Banishing Pentagrams as those used by Mathers and his followers, but drawn upside down; according to Lévi such a Pentagram was a symbol of black magic, symbolising the triumph of matter over spirit, and, certainly, most occultists regard the inverted Pentagram as pertaining to the world of devils rather than to the angelic kingdoms. Similarly, Russell taught the OTOs sexual magic, but with some curious variations of his own – notably the preliminary practice of Alphaism (i.e. complete chastity) and the replacement of the 'magical masturbation' of the OTO by Karezza, prolonged sexual intercourse without orgasm. This, the GBG taught, should be persisted in until one or both participants in the act reached the 'borderland state', a sort of hallucinatory trance in which the magician sees his or her sexual partner as an aspect of the 'Holy Guardian Angel'. The highest grade of the order practised normal heterosexual activities, using the psychic energies they believed to be released by these to obtain both mystic illuminations and material benefits.

In 1938 the GBG was officially either closed down or put into abeyance by its founder. One of his pupils, however, a professional astrologer named Louis T. Culling, continued to operate at least one GBG lodge. Mr. Culling also headed the Order of the Reformed Palladium, a mysterious secret society with a charter which bore the (forged) signature of Wynn Westcott of the Golden Dawn. In the late '60s and early '70s Mr. Culling published a number of books on sexual magic, including a sexual interpretation of the Chinese *I Ching*, and interested himself in psychic aphrodisiacs. These are substances which are believed not only to arouse the libidos of those who consume them but also to magically attract the right partners to satisfy those libidos.

The magic herb which particularly aroused Mr. Culling's interest was damiana, a fragrant shrub which grows widely throughout California, Texas and Mexico; its leaves can be dried and used as a *tisane*, or smoked in a pipe, or even infused in brandy and drunk as a tonic.

Mr. Culling began his experimenting with damiana in 1962, when he was 69 years of age. Each day he boiled two large spoonfuls of the dried leaves in a cupful of water, allowed the portion to cool and then drank it. Ten days of this and the first results became apparent; women twenty and thirty years younger than himself began to 'take an interest' in him.

A few days later he set off for a short holiday in the Mexican border town of Tijuana. Here he quickly became acquainted with a 33 year old waitress who agreed to visit him in his hotel room. Her first visit, for which Mr. Culling prepared himself by drinking a pint of damiana-flavoured liqueur, and those that followed it, proved satisfactory to both parties. The friends of the waitress noted that she had 'stars in her eyes', while the near septuagenarian sex magician conducted himself in a manner creditable in a man of any age; or so Mr. Culling reported in his book *Sex Magick*.

In the 1940s Mr. Culling was on friendly terms with OTO magicians of a more authentically 'Crowleyan' variety than those with whom he had been associated in the GBG. These were members of the Californian Agapé lodge of the OTO.

This had been founded by W.T. Smith, a member of the order since 1915 and, it will be remembered, C.S. Jones' successor as chief of the North American OTO – an organisation which hardly existed between 1920 and *circa* 1935.

In the mid-thirties Smith moved to California and was given a job by the Southern Californian Gas Company, probably as the result of the recommendation of a fellow-member of the OTO already in the employment of that body. Shortly afterwards the gaseous magicians founded the Agapé lodge and began to actively propagate Crowley's Magick in general and OTO sex magic in particular. Soon there were approaching a hundred members of the lodge and Smith began to carry out public celebrations of the Gnostic Mass. This last was an error; reporters began to attend the Mass and to take an interest in the personal and occult activities of Smith. Neither could stand close examination and a devastating newspaper exposure followed. Smith almost lost his job and three quarters of Agapé initiates resigned from the lodge.

The Californian OTO was saved from extinction by a new recruit, Jack Parsons, who joined it in 1939. Parsons, born in 1914, was a fervent admirer of Crowley and an enthusiastic practitioner of sexual magic. He persuaded Smith of the desirability of establishing an 'Abbey of Thelema' – a sort of OTO commune – and the two occultists rented an enormous house and moved into it with a dozen or so of their fellow magicians.

Personal relationships soon caused trouble and Parsons' wife transferred her affections to Smith and bore him a child. Smith, perhaps because of his difficulties with Parsons, spent little time at the 'Abbey' and, when he was there, administered it in an unintelligent way.

Crowley, directing his followers by postal communications from England, became concerned and investigated the situation by the curious device of casting Smith's horoscope. The conclusion he arrived at was a surprising one. W.T. Smith was not a human being, but the incarnation of a god; which god was uncertain – perhaps, mused Crowley, some Red Indian deity . . .

In any case W.T. Smith must forthwith become only nominally the leader of the Agapé lodge of the OTO, handing it over to Parsons, and go on a 'Great Magical Retirement'. This would supposedly reveal to Smith his real, divine identity. Smith carried out his chief's instructions. Alas, however, far from any apotheosis taking place he suffered some sort of psychological breakdown. Before retiring into obscurity he described his condition in a bitterly unhappy letter to Crowley:

> . . . I am completely empty; so much so I do not know whether I write accurately about myself. In fact I don't know anything at all. . . . I have ill understood your dealings with me these many years, and I am no better informed at this moment.

Meanwhile a new magician appeared on the scene. We shall call him Frater Scire. Exactly why he became involved with the OTO is uncertain. Possibly he was, for a time at least, converted to Crowley's Magick. According to his own account, however, he was acting as an agent for the FBI, who sent him into the Agapé lodge in order that he might 'destroy the menace of black magic in California'.

Parsons was particularly impressed with the psychic abilities of Frater Scire. On one occasion, for example, Scire clairvoyantly discerned the astral body of Smith sneaking into Parsons' room, presumably with the intention of attacking him. Scire included amongst his many accomplishments the art of knife-throwing; he pinned the ghostly Smith to the door with a dagger. Parsons, who was not clairvoyantly gifted had to take Scire's word for this. Later that night, however, he heard a faint voice crying 'Let me go free'; Parsons recited a magical formula designed to release the imprisoned spirit and quietness resumed.

Frater Scire and Parsons extended their collaboration from magic to money. They set up a joint financial operation – 'Allied Enterprises' – to which Parsons contributed most of the money. A complicated series of events followed which ended with Parsons almost penniless and Frater Scire in possession of – no doubt quite legally – a large yacht, some money, and Parsons' girlfriend.

Parsons employed his magical knowledge against his former friend, evoking Bartzabel, the spirit of Mars, so successfully that the yacht had its sails torn off in a squall off Miami and was forced to return to port. This success was only temporary. Scire eventually succeeded in parting company with Parsons and achieved fame in many other fields than magic – inventing an anti-radiation compound, growing gigantic tomatoes, and curing people of life-long sinus infections, for example.

Parsons too had his triumphs. He became a scientist of distinction – a lunar crater is named after him – and did much of the basic research work on rocket fuels which ultimately led to the success of the American Apollo programme.

His unfortunate experiences, financial and emotional,

did not end his interest in magic. In 1946, for example, he embarked upon a series of complex rituals designed to achieve the birth of a child who would be an incarnation of the Scarlet Woman of the *Apocalypse*. Crowley was not impressed; he remarked to another disciple: 'I get fairly frantic when I contemplate the idiocy of these louts.'

Crowley died in 1947, so we do not know what he would have thought of the later occult doings of Parsons; of, for example, his legally changing his name to Belarion Armilus Al Dajjal Anti-Christ.

Until Parsons' death in a laboratory explosion in 1952 the Agapé lodge continued a shadowy existence and various attempts were made to attract new recruits – a correspondence course in 'witchcraft' was advertised, for example. This witchcraft was of a somewhat different nature from the modern witchcraft which we shall be describing in a later chapter. Indeed, for Parsons witchcraft was no more than a slightly watered-down version of the orgiastic occult theology of the OTO. In a 'preliminary instruction' on witchcraft, possibly written by him, it is said:

> We are the oldest religion in the world, and the strongest. We were with the first man and we shall be with the last. . . . Long ago . . . man became separated from us. . . . From the life and love of our living religion, he turned to dead gods. . . . He made demons and infused them with the breath of his life. . . . We waited, suffering the flames of the stake, the rack, the lash – carrying in our hearts the secret seed that could, in its hour, redeem the world. . . . On mountains and secret heaths, in lonely and desolate places we gathered the covens of The Witchcraft. We held the Agapé love feasts. . . . In fairy tales and playing cards, in myths and legends . . . we hid the secret knowledge. . . . We are come to make a door out of hell; to gather the elect before the Days of Wrath. . . . We have knowledge that will save a damned soul out of the lowest hell. . . .

After Crowley's death the world leader of the OTO –

the 'Outer Head of the Order' – was Karl Germer, who also inherited Crowley's papers and magical robes. Germer, a German who had moved to New York after suffering persecution at the hands of the Nazis, was not a particularly effective chief. Partly this was because of his personality; he was both autocratic with and suspicious of, other occultists. Partly because, living on the East Coast, he was cut off from both the Californian OTO and the isolated individuals and groups who were situated in Europe. He did, however, charter a Swiss section of the OTO which flourished throughout the 1950s and 60s, publishing German translations of many of Crowley's books. Of late years this organisation seems to have experienced some financial difficulties and to have become less active.

At about the same time there was a small revival of sexual magic in Germany and 'Gregor A. Gregorius' of Saturn-Gnosis, mentioned by us previously, resumed his activities. These were regarded with disapproval by Karl Germer.

For some years following the death of Jack Parsons the only really active OTO magicians in California were a follower of Crowley named Grady McMurtry and his immediate associates. Mr. McMurtry had received a 'charter' from Crowley in March 1946 at the time of the upheavals in the Agapé lodge. This appointed him Crowley's 'Caliph' – i.e. spiritual representative:

> This is to authorize Frater Hymanaeus Alpha (Captain Grady L. McMurtry) to take charge of the whole work of the Order in California . . . subject to the approval of Frater Saturnus [Karl Germer]. . . .

Crowley amplified this authorization in the following month:

> . . . These presents are to appoint . . . Grady Louis McMurtry IX° OTO as our representative in the United States of America and his authority is to be considered as Ours, subject to the approval, revision or veto of our Viceroy Karl Johannes Germer . . .

It seems likely that Mr. McMurtry, an occultist possessed of both literary and organizing ability, would have succeeded in rebuilding the American OTO in the period 1952–62 if it had not been for Karl Germer, who not only failed to name an heir-apparent as head of the OTO but refused to allow any new initiations into the higher grades of the order.

Germer died in 1962. Since then, as will be mentioned in the next chapter, OTO-derived sexual magic has become widespread amongst both European and American occultists.

13 The Magical Explosion

It is only since the 1950s that the Western magical revival, that long drawn out process of occult evolution begun by Eliphas Lévi over a century and a quarter ago, has come to the attention of the general public. Over the last 25 or so years there has been an occult boom, a 'magical explosion', of a sort not experienced since the later years of the Roman Empire. To give a detailed account of this cultural revolution would require many thousands – perhaps many tens of thousands – of words. All that we can even begin to do in one short chapter is to outline the achievements of some of those contemporary occultists who have either played a major part in the occult revival or, in one way or another, typify certain aspects of it.

That the rebirth of occult magic has taken place in the way it has can be very largely attributed to the writings of one man, Dr. Francis Israel Regardie. It is not, of course, that all magicians approve of Dr. Regardie and his opinions – indeed some of them have an antipathetic attitude towards him and them. Nevertheless, there would be far, far fewer practising Western occultists working in either the Golden Dawn or 'Crowleyan' traditions if Dr. Regardie had never written any books.

Israel Regardie was born in 1907 of Jewish parents living in London's East End. While still a child he was taken to the USA, although even today his accent bears some traces of his Anglo-Jewish origins, and here he read and was captivated by Crowley's *Equinox*.

He wrote to Crowley, received friendly replies, and in

1928 returned to Europe to become the magician's private secretary and occult pupil.

At the time Crowley was, from the occult point of view, fairly inactive; he was too busy attempting to get enough funds to live on, publishing and selling copies of his *magnum opus, Magick in Theory and Practice*, and writing letters to his scattered disciples, to be able to give Regardie the *practical* instructions in ritual magic which the latter desired. Nevertheless the young American put his years with Crowley to good use, acquiring a profound knowledge of the Golden Dawn magical and qabalistic systems.

Crowley had always wanted to write books on magic which could be read and understood by the ordinary reader. He never succeeded in doing this, although he made several efforts to do so. He wrote with great clarity and simplicity on yoga, but his purely magical writings are largely incomprehensible to the reader not equipped with a detailed knowledge of Mathers's qabalism, the rites of the Golden Dawn, and even the events of Crowley's own life.

The pupil succeeded where the master had failed. In 1932 Regardie published two books, the *Tree of Life* and *The Garden of Pomegranates*, which many consider to be minor occult masterpieces. The former work dealt with the techniques of ritual magic, the latter with the qabalah; in spite of Regardie's close relationship with Crowley they represent the pure Golden Dawn system rather than 'Crowleyanity'. It would seem that, young as he was, Regardie had the discrimination to discern which particular elements of 'Magick' were drawn from, respectively, the OTO, from the *Book of the Law*, and from the Golden Dawn. The *Tree of Life* gives, using alchemical symbolism, a detailed account of the 'Mass of the Holy Ghost' – in other words, the sexual magic of the OTO.

Regardie's revelations met with a mixed response. A representative of the Alpha et Omega, Captain E.J. Langford-Garstin, wrote to him demanding that he should never again mention the name of the Golden Dawn in print; occult secrecy, he affirmed, was all-important. Dion

Fortune took the opposite point of view, greeting Regardie's books with enthusiasm and arguing that much occult secrecy was unnecessary. A representative of the Stella Matutina, presumably a schizophrenic, managed to hold both points of view at the same time and wrote to both Langford-Garstin and Dion Fortune expressing full agreement with their respective positions. Unfortunately the letters were inserted in the wrong envelopes . . .

When writing his books Regardie had assumed that the Golden Dawn and its derivatives were defunct. He discovered his mistake when he met some representatives of the Stella Matutina, notably a Mrs. Hughes, and in 1934 he was admitted into the order, making rapid progress through its grades and acquiring an even fuller knowledge of Mathers' system than that which he had derived from Crowley.

He was not particularly impressed with most of the initiates he met. They made claim to hold fantastically high occult grades, claims which, in Regardie's own words, 'set a gigantic question mark against the validity of their attainment' but seemed to have failed to have fully understood the complexities of Mathers' system. Even more alarmingly they were engaging in an unintelligent tampering with the system, withdrawing some instructional manuscripts from circulation and revising others in accordance with their own inclinations. Regardie, who regarded the Golden Dawn's synthetic version of the western esoteric tradition as being of great spiritual value, decided to break the oaths of secrecy he had taken and to make Mathers' rituals and occult instructions available to all. After all, he argued, they had already been published in a condensed form in the pages of Crowley's *Equinox*.

Between 1938 and 1940 the Aries Press of Chicago published four volumes of Golden Dawn material edited by Regardie. Except for some minor omissions, notably the side-lectures known as Flying Rolls, these contained all the material circulated in the pre-1900 Golden Dawn. For many years, in spite – or perhaps because – of its excellence, this compilation sold very slowly. Almost twenty years after its first publication it was still in print and was available from London's leading occult bookseller.

In the early 1950s there was a mild revival of interest in ritual magic, presumably sparked off by the publication of John Symond's biography and C.R. Cammell's memoir of Aleister Crowley. The price of second-hand copies of the latter's books began to rise and individual occultists began to experiment with the techniques taught in those books. Some of these latter found the traditional Western magic embedded in Crowley's system to be of more interest to them than either OTO sex magic or the new religion of Thelema and diverted their attention to the Golden Dawn. They studied Regardie's writings and more popular occult manuals which taught simplified Golden Dawn techniques, such as those written by the late W.E. Butler, a one-time pupil of Dion Fortune.

Eventually these individual practitioners of ceremonial magic began to come together and form new occult brotherhoods in both Britain and the USA. Sometimes such fraternities have claimed to be 'derived from the Golden Dawn' or 'older than the Golden Dawn', but not one of them has produced evidence to satisfactorily confirm these claims. It is probable, therefore, that they are all based on literary sources – primarily the writings of Israel Regardie. This does not mean, of course, that what is taught by these organisations is valueless, nor that they do not number amongst their members occultists who have travelled far along the road of magical attainment.

All occultists tend to be eclectic; they refuse to rigidly study and practise one esoteric system but rather create a personal synthesis in which one system is enriched by elements derived from others. Present-day magicians working in the Golden Dawn tradition have been no exception to this rule, and techniques and theories drawn from such diverse sources as tantric yoga, Jungian analytical psychology, and the 'orgonomic functionalism' of Wilhelm Reich have been incorporated into Western magic by one group or another. A system which has particularly intrigued such eclectics is that which was evolved, largely on the basis of his own psychic intuitions, by the eccentric but talented artist Austin Spare.

Spare was born in 1889, the son of a London policeman, was for a brief period a member of the 'Silver Star', Aleister Crowley's magical order, and some of his drawings appeared in the *Equinox*; they illustrated, for example, the instructional article on the method of divination known as geomancy.

While still an adolescent Spare became friendly with an elderly fortune-teller, a Mrs. Paterson, whom he believed to be an 'hereditary witch' and whom he claimed to have seen transform herself at will from an aged woman to a beautiful young girl. It was she who first aroused his interest in the magical arts – not surprisingly if, as Spare asserted, he had seen her demonstrate the power to 'materialize thought'; that is, to think of something and to simultaneously induce in other persons the illusion that they saw it physically present before them.

Spare invented his own version of (male) sexual magic which has intrigued some magicians but to others has appeared ludicrous. It involves the manufacture of a vase with a neck which exactly fits the erect phallus of the operator. In the body of the vase is placed a piece of parchment or paper inscribed with a sigil – or occult diagram – expressing in symbolic form the particular wish of the magician. He then uses the vase as an artificial vagina, at the moment of orgasm visualising the desired result as strongly as he can. The vase, with its 'consecrated sigil', must then be sealed during the moon's first quarter.

The sigils used by Spare for this and similar purposes were constructed by a method of his own devising. A sentence expressing some desired result or event was written down in the briefest possible form. All letters which duplicated earlier letters in the sentence and, sometimes, all vowels were crossed out; then the remaining letters were combined, much after the manner of a Victorian monogram, to form the sigil.

One of the ways in which these 'Sparean' sigils are used

by contemporary magicians is as follows. The sigil is stared at by the occultist until its form, and the desire it symbolically expresses, fills his entire consciousness and 'overflows' into the depths of the unconscious. Then the desire is deliberately forgotten and only the sigil stripped of its significance is held in the mind. The 'It' – the deepest and most primitive component of the unconscious – is then left to work on the sigil. As the 'It' is supposedly possessed of supernormal powers, untapped by the ordinary human being whose conscious thinking blocks the 'It' from achieving its full potential, it can manipulate the occultist's environment to 'materialise' the wish embodied in the sigil.

Spare held that self-exhaustion could be used as a means of magically obtaining one's desires. By the deliberate creation, he argued, of mental or spiritual emptiness, a sort of psychological vacuum, it was possible to attract a desired reality by supplying a 'space' which it could fill. He extended this method of 'occult voidness' to a technique designed to turn bitter disappointments to personal advantage. The idea was to use the ending of belief in some theory, institution or person, to absorb the *mana*, the magical and psychological power, which had become associated with and enshrined in that belief. If, for example, one ceased to believe in the truth of Marx's theory of surplus value one should absorb all the 'emotional charge' that has become attached to that theory in the course of a century or more of agitation and revolution.

Spare's assertion of the positive magical values of disappointment and disillusion if they were handled in the appropriate way was paralleled by his belief that the emotions of revulsion and disgust could be used advantageously by the occultist. This was particularly the case, so he said, where aesthetics were concerned in sexual matters. Fixed ideas of the 'beautiful' and the 'good', as distinct from the 'ugly' and 'bad', serve to imprison the It and to cut the individual off from 'new pleasures without fear'; this can be overcome by sexual union with those whose physical appearance one finds grotesque or repellent.

A curious self-portrait by Austin Spare, showing the artist as dreamer and magician. (Pen drawing by Austin Spare, 1907.)

Spare also believed in the magical value of a state of vacuity achieved by means of what he called 'the death posture'. His teachings concerning this are involved and obscure and are best approached through the study of his own writings and drawings, notably those contained in *The Book of Pleasure*. An excellent introduction to the study of these is provided in the two chapters devoted to Spare in Mr. Kenneth Grant's *The Magical Revival* (1972).

This and other more recent magical studies written by Mr. Grant have strongly influenced a number of occultists and always make interesting, if sometimes difficult, reading.

Mr. Grant is an admirer of Aleister Crowley and his Magick, although his interpretation of the latter is considered highly unorthodox by a number of fellow believers in Crowleyanity. When only a young man he began corresponding with the Master Therion, as Crowley sometimes called himself, and in 1945 spent some time with him in Hastings. Here, under, Crowley's tuition, Mr. Grant practised the 'symbolic door' method of astral projection described by us in an earlier chapter, intensifying his experiences by inhaling ether.

In 1951 or 1952 Karl Germer, the German-American occultist who had succeeded Crowley as chief of the OTO, gave Mr. Grant a limited charter to operate a lodge working the first three degrees of the OTO. All went well until in 1955 Mr. Grant expanded his activities, announcing the formation of 'New Isis Lodge O.T.O.' in a manifesto which met with Germer's disapproval.

The manifesto was written in a guarded and sometimes obscure style. As far as we can understand it suggests a new interpretation of – or, perhaps, a revelation concerning – the first chapter of Crowley's *Book of the Law*. This was in some way connected with the belief that, far beyond the orbit of Pluto, is a tenth planet called Isis. It is perhaps worth remarking that, while some have suspected that there might be a trans-Plutonian planet and have even, by an extension of Bode's Law, worked out a hypothetical orbit for it, there is so far no astronomical evidence for its existence. Germer, who saw himself as the guardian of Crowleyan orthodoxy, was infuriated by these hints concerning an occult wisdom unknown to either Crowley or himself. He was also annoyed by a friendly reference to 'the Master G∴' who was to undertake the Saturnian element of a revelation concerning the *Book of the Law*; the Master G∴ was none other than 'Gregor A. Gregorius', the chief of Saturn Gnosis who, it will be remembered, was not one of Germer's favourite magicians.

Mr. Grant composed eleven rituals for the lodge – one for group working and ten for initiation ceremonies – which he declined to send to Germer for examination and possible official authorisation. An acrimonious correspondence followed in which Germer expressed his dislike of Gregor A. Gregorius and Mr. Grant his low opinion of Herr Metzger, chief of the Swiss OTO. Eventually, on 20 July 1955, Germer sent Mr. Grant a letter which withdrew his authority to operate a 'Camp' of the OTO and purported to expel him from the order. Whether or not Karl Germer was entitled to expel individuals from the OTO we are unaware. Clearly, however, Mr. Grant thought not, for he continued to run his occult society and in recent years has not only asserted that he is a member of the OTO but has claimed to be the 'O.H.O.' – the Outer Head of the Order.

Karl Germer was not the only occultist to have disagreements with Mr. Grant, for it would seem that the late Gerald Gardner – a 'witch' whose activities are described in some detail in our next chapter – actually went to the lengths of launching a magical attack upon him.

This attack was described by Mr. Grant on the back page of No. 30 of the partwork *Man, Myth and Magic*. It began by Gerald Gardner suspecting, no doubt quite wrongly, that Mr. Grant was 'stealing' his witches. His resentment was particularly aroused when one of his disciples, a young woman who called herself a 'water witch', became magically involved with Mr. Grant's New Isis Lodge. Lacking, it is to be presumed, confidence in his own occult abilities, Gardner got Austin Spare to manufacture a talisman intended to restore 'stolen property' to its rightful owner. Into this talisman Spare bound, so he asserted, a demon of an unusual nature – an 'amphibious owl with the wings of a bat and the talons of an eagle'.

At the time the initiates of New Isis Lodge, who knew nothing of the preparation of Spare's sinister charm nor what end it was intended to achieve, were holding their meetings in an old and semi-derelict house, the property of a furrier with alchemical inclinations who has since written rather a good book on the 'hermetic art' from the point of view of a practising alchemist.

One evening the alleged water witch was the focus of a rite being performed in the alchemist's house – an invocation of the Black Isis. She lay on an altar while 'magnetic passes' were made over her body. Suddenly she sat upright, apparently terror-stricken. Simultaneously, the room chilled and a sinister scratching – perhaps the sound of giant talons – was heard from outside the curtained window.

Then, invisible to all save the water witch, a huge bird flew into the room, seized her (astral) body in its claws, and carried her out over the streets of London. She struggled to get free, felt herself falling, and then found herself back in her physical body, still lying on the altar. On the window the alarmed magicians found the imprint of giant claws and a pullulating green jelly. This last turned first to slime and then evaporated, leaving behind only a strong smell of the sea.

There, as far as we are aware, the occult attack terminated.

Mr. Grant is numbered amongst those contemporary magicians who regard the supernatural fiction of the late H.P. Lovecraft as being of occult significance. Lovecraft himself would have been surprised by this, for, as is revealed by his correspondence, he was a confirmed rationalist and agnostic who believed all occultists to be 'crackpots'. Nevertheless, a number of occultists have come to the conclusion that Lovecraft, perhaps through dreams, had achieved a psychic awareness of non-human entities and their activities and in his fiction expressed profound esoteric truths, albeit distorted through the prism of his own rationality. Thus Mr. Grant has asserted his belief that at least some of Lovecraft's fantasy reflects 'the salient themes of Crowley's Cult'.

A magician who shares this belief is the Chicago-born American occultist Michael Bertiaux (born 1935) who is 'High Priest of the Cult of the Black Snake' – a voodoo/magical cult which supposedly has its headquarters in Haiti – the chief of the 'Monastery of the Seven Rays', which conducts correspondence courses in magic and seems to be an outer court of the Black Snake Cult, and a leading adept of a fraternity called 'the Ancient Order of Eastern Templars', of which we know nothing except that it accepts the theology of Aleister Crowley's *Book of the Law*.

The system taught by Mr. Bertiaux incorporates aspects of voodoo, particularly the cult of the dead, of Indian tantricism, of Western magic, and even, it is claimed, 'Red and Black Temple Atlantean Magic'. Mr. Bertiaux would also seem to have invented various occult machines which, Mr. Kenneth Grant has asserted, receive impulses from areas of space beyond the orbit of Neptune and transmit 'mysterious and outlandish music'. The most astonishing and, no doubt, useful of Mr. Bertiaux's devices is the Zothyriometre, which projects magical force to any chosen area of the astral plane . . .

A sub-division of the Cult of the Black Snake is the 'Lovecraftian Coven', which is particularly concerned with the 'Deep Ones' – non-human but intelligent entities, the product of Lovecraft's literary imagination, who are supposedly particularly associated with the world's lakes and seas. Mr. Bertiaux seems to believe in the actual existence of these creatures; at a Wisconsin lake shore he and a group of his associates have carried out ceremonies designed to evoke the Deep Ones. These rites involve priest and priestess standing in the waters of the lake and there carrying out a 'transference of sex-magical energy'. This, it is almost needless to say, is only done when the astrological conditions are suitable, i.e. when the sun is in a watery sign of the Zodiac.

Another American-based occult organization which has been influenced by the Cthulu-mythos – the quite imaginary myths and legends invented by Lovecraft as a conceptual framework for his fiction – is the Church of Satan, headed by Anton La Vey.

Mr. La Vey, who was at one time a circus performer and has continued to keep up his links with show business – he played the Devil in the film of *Rosemary's Baby* – has combined a flair for publicity with the authorship and compilation of some intensely readable books. These, notably the *Satanic Bible* and the *Satanic Rituals*, show not only a detailed knowledge of the byways of literature, from the obscure writings of Aleister Crowley to tracts written by late Victorian individualist anarchists, but a talent approaching genius for the composition of impressive – and, no doubt, psychologically effective – ceremonies.

These rites are based on a more catholic use of symbol-systems than that employed by most Western magicians of the present day. Thus the ceremony known as *Das Tierdrama* incorporates material identical with passages in H.G. Wells's *Island of Dr. Moreau*, while *Die Elektrischen Vorspiele* contains elements drawn from such diverse sources as the magic of the Golden Dawn, early science fantasy and even the symbolism popular with the early Nazis. Mr. La Vey's Lovecraftian enthusiasms are made apparent in his 'Ceremony of the Nine Angles' and his 'Call to Cthulu'.

These latter ceremonies do not pretend to be anything but recent in origin; some magicians, however, have become so obsessed with Lovecraft's 'Cthulu-mythos' that in recent years a number of spoof, or 'forged', versions of the *Necronomicon* – Lovecraft's imagined grimoire – have been produced.

The most amusing of these is perhaps that originally

published by Neville Spearman (Jersey) Ltd. in 1978. The core of this is a 'grimoire', which clearly incorporates many key phrases from Lovecraft's fiction, researched by Mr. Robert Turner, who is himself a practising magician and was – and perhaps still is – one of the chiefs of an occult fraternity called the Order of the Cubic Stone.

Another occultist who has been associated with the Cubic Stone is David Edwards, the author of a Do-It-Yourself occult manual entitled *Dare to Make Magic*; this has been criticised on stylistic grounds but many of those who have followed its instructions have found it useful. The ideological stance adopted by the author – an intelligent but not slavish adherence to Mathers' system – typifies that of many present day magicians. Some Crowleyan influences on Mr. Edwards are apparent in his book, and there are few western magicians totally uninfluenced by Crowley and his writings.

Occultists who take their inspiration almost entirely from Crowley's Magick are to be found throughout Europe and America. Perhaps the most 'orthodox' of these are to be found in the ranks of Mr. Grady McMurtry's OTO. This fraternity, whose origins we described in our last chapter, has taken on a new lease of life in recent years. It has an intelligent and growing membership and produces a really excellent (and extremely forthright!) magazine.

There are at the present day, then, magicians who take their inspiration from the Golden Dawn, from Crowley, from Lovecraft, and from a wide variety of sources mixed with all of these.

There are also, as we shall see, witches.

14 Witches

In 1967 the then Duke of Leinster became worried about the declining fortunes of his family, the result, the Duke believed, of a curse. He inserted an advertisement in the personal column of *The Times*; 'A witch of full powers is urgently sought to lift a 73-year-old curse and help restore the family fortunes of an afflicted nobleman. Employment genuinely offered'.

The advertisement attracted a good many 'witches', all of whom supposed they had 'full powers'. One of them was a distant cousin of the Duke of Norfolk. Most of them, however, were less aristocratic, for as Frank Smyth has remarked:

> The habitat of the average witch is . . . cosy and mundane. . . .Semis, red-brick Edwardian terraced houses, and flats in the suburbs are . . . the usual scene of coven meetings. . . .The decor of the typical witch's home tends to reflect . . . love of elaborate ornament . . . crystal balls, Maori spears, and ritual swords and daggers all jostle for pride of place among Tretchikoff prints and formations of plaster ducks.

Exactly how many people in Britain and North America are members of witchcraft groups – 'covens' – is uncertain. Estimates vary between 'a few hundred' and 'a few hundred thousand', and it seems reasonably certain that the true figure lies somewhere between these extremes.

Modern witches believe themselves to be practitioners

of the ancient fertility religion of Stone-Age Europe. This religion, they assert, has never died. In the Middle Ages, subjected to the persecution of the Church, it went underground, its devotees regarded as 'devil worshippers'. Now, in a more tolerant age, they can be more open about their activities, publicly expounding their beliefs and casting spells for healing and other beneficial purposes.

It is remotely possible that this is true. All the evidence, however, would seem to show that modern witchcraft has no real 'apostolic succession' from the ancient or mediaeval worlds and that it must be regarded as no more than one of the many new religio-magical cults which have proliferated in recent years. This does not mean to say, of course, that witchcraft is not of great psychological and even spiritual value to those who take part in its rites, nor that its doctrines, and the legends which incorporate them, do not express what C.G. Jung called 'psychic truths'.

We know nothing for certain of the religious and magical beliefs and practices of our Stone-Age ancestors. From what little evidence we have – for example stone images of pregnant women with grossly enlarged sexual organs – and from intelligent guesswork based on what we know of primitive peoples who have survived into modern times, we can surmise that these beliefs and practices were concerned with sex and fertility. When, therefore, present-day witches affirm that they are practising a prehistoric religion outsiders can only shrug their shoulders and say: 'It seems unlikely, but it just may be so.'

What of the witches of three, four and five centuries ago? The men and women who appeared in the ecclesiastical and civil courts and confessed, often with a wealth of circumstantial detail, to attending 'Sabbaths', orgiastic celebrations of the 'Old Religion' of sex and fertility. Surely modern witches have some historical links with these?

Alas, in spite of all that has been written by such writers as Margaret Murray and Hugh Ross Williamson, it seems probable that no Witches' Sabbath ever took place, that there was never any such thing as an organised witch cult before the present century. For, as Norman Cohn has shown beyond all reasonable doubt in his *Europe's Inner Demons*, the idea of the existence of a witch cult, a rival and diabolic religion opposed to Christianity, was a fantasy born in the minds of late mediaeval ecclesiastics and based on confused notions about both ritual magic and the nature of dualistic heresies such as that of the Cathars. Without exception all the early cases which supposedly illustrate the existence of a witch religion turn out, on close examination, to be either cases of ordinary heresy, or of ritual magic, or of *maleficum*, an individual casting evil spells. There were, it is true, individuals who in the 16th and 17th centuries confessed to attending meetings of witches and there taking part in the worship of a 'horned God' – the Christian Devil. However, as those same individuals also confessed to such unlikely feats as physical flight and visits to fairyland there is no reason to believe the truth of such admissions.

All that we definitely know of the origins of modern witchcraft is that few people even suspected the cult's existence before 1954, the year in which the late Gerald Gardner published his book *Witchcraft Today*.

Gardner, born in 1884, spent most of his adult life in the Far East, working as a planter and, latterly, as a customs official. He was fascinated by edged weapons, had a large collection of them, and wrote a monograph on the Malayan *kris*. He was also extremely interested in naturism, folk-lore, bondage and, above all, occultism. This latter led him to make some unusual friends, amongst them J.S.M. Ward, a self-appointed Abbot who ran an eccentric religious community, 'The Abbey of Christ the King', which had moved from England to Cyprus after encountering legal difficulties. It was possibly from Ward, concerned in the affairs of more than one bogus 'university', that Gardner acquired the various doctorates he claimed to possess. Another friend was Aleister Crowley who, in return for a substantial fee, chartered Gardner as head of an OTO lodge.

Shortly before World War II Gardner would seem to have been admitted to membership of some sort of witch coven operating in the New Forest area of Hampshire. The late Louis Wilkinson claimed to have independently come into contact with this group, so there is no need to doubt that it existed – although whether its origins were as ancient as its leaders claimed is doubtful.

By 1954 Gardner was in touch with covens in 'the North, South, East, and West of England' – cultists who authorised him to give an account of their beliefs in his *Witchcraft Today*. The central message of the book was given in the form of alleged quotations from practising witches. One of them summarised witch beliefs as follows:

> Our gods . . . . desire good to us, fertility for man, beast and crops. . . . When we die we go to the gods' domain, where having rested a while in their lovely country we are prepared to be born again on this earth; and if we perform the rites correctly, by the grace of the Great Mother we will be reborn among those we loved, and will remember, know and love them again. . . . Being reborn again we ever progress. . . . What we endure here in this life fits us for better in the next. . . . Thus the gods teach us to look forward to the time when we be not men any more, when we become one with the Mighty Ones.

In other words, the witches with whom Gerald Gardner was in contact believed in reincarnation. This in itself is enough to make it seem highly probable that their cult was of comparatively recent origin. For, while certain mediaeval dualists believed in a modified form of the transmigration of souls, there is no trace of the doctrine of reincarnation having been associated with post-classical western occultism before 1875.

The witch quoted above went on to describe the nature of the cult's religious activities:

> Ours is a religion of love, pleasure and excitement. Frail human nature needs a little warmth and comfort, to

> relieve us from the hardness and misery of life and from the cold austerity of the Church's preaching – comfort on earth, not in some far-distant paradise beyond the grave. We worship the divine spirit of Creation, which is the Life-Spring of the world and without which the world would perish. To us it is the most sacred and holy mystery, proof that God is within us whose command is: 'Go forth and multiply'. Such rites are done in a holy and reverent way.

What seems to be meant in the above quotation, when the pious verbiage is stripped away, is that the witch cult is concerned with fertility and that its religio-magical rites are concerned with sex.

At the time he wrote Gardner considered that the witchcraft he knew would soon die a natural death. Science, he remarked, had displaced the witch:

> . . . good weather reports, good health services, outdoor games, bathing, nudism, the cinema and television have largely replaced what the witch had to give. Free thought or spiritualism, according to your inclinations, have taken away the fear of Hell that she prevented, though nothing, yet, has replaced her greatest gifts: peace, joy and content.

But *Witchcraft Today* attracted a surprisingly large number of readers, probably because of the coverage it received in a popular Sunday newspaper. Most of its readers were only mildly interested in the supposed revelations it contained, but some were sufficiently enthusiastic about the book to write to its author asking how they too could share in the 'peace, joy and content' of witchcraft.

Most of Gardner's correspondents were given a polite brush-off. Some of them, however, he initiated into witchcraft by rites which he said were traditional. These involved nudity, some mild scourging, and a certain amount of esoteric flim-flam – nothing any rational person could take any great objection to.

Following their initiations the new witches were handed

a manuscript copy of the *Book of Shadows*, supposedly the ancient instructional manual of the cult, and told to copy it out in their own 'hand of write'.

The *Book of Shadows* is partly written in a pseudo-archaic English – 'Sight cometh to divers people in different ways' is a fair example – but its modern origins are apparent. Take, for example, the instructions for the festival cult members should celebrate on 'August Eve'. This begins:

> Proceed to the Rite riding brooms and staves using a quick dance step. The High Priestess leads carrying a wand. The High Priest follows behind, others following, all singing:-
>
> *O do not tell the priest our Art,*
> *For he would call it sin,*
> *For we'll be in the woods all night,*
> *A-Conjuring harvest in.*
> *And we bring you good news by word of mouth*
> *For Women, Cattle and Corn,*
> *Now the Sun has come up from the south,*
> *With oak and ash and thorn.*

The song has a folksy authenticity about it. Actually, however, it is a slightly modified version of a poem by Rudyard Kipling.

Again, take the instructions for 'getting the sight', i.e. astral visions:

> . . . In the Craft we are taught . . . to intensify the imagination at the same time controlling the blood supply . . . The circle being formed and everything being properly prepared the aspirant should first bind and then take the teacher into the circle . . . then he should lightly use the scourge. Then the teacher in turn should bind the aspirant . . . enough to retard the blood slightly . . . the teacher should use the scourge with light, steady strokes. . . . It is very important that the pupil should see the strokes coming as this . . . greatly stimulates the imagination. . . . This, with the light

binding, slows down the circulation of the blood . . . as soon as the aspirant speaks or sleeps the scourging should stop. . . . Be not discouraged if no results come at the first attempt, results usually occur after two or three attempts. . . . It has been found that this practice doth often cause a fondness between aspirant and teacher . . . and it is for this reason that a man may only be taught by a woman and a woman by a man; and that man and man and woman and woman should never attempt these practices together. May the curse of the Mighty Ones be on such as make the attempt.

Whether or not the techniques described above have ever induced clairvoyance – 'the sight' – is not known to us. What does seem likely from the tone of the instructions, and from the remarks about 'a fondness between aspirant and teacher', is that they were written by someone, perhaps Gardner himself, with a sexual interest in bondage and flagellation. Sexual motives, possibly of a voyeuristic nature, would also seem to have been responsible for the incorporation into the *Book of Shadows* of a 'Conjuration of Diana'. This begins by a witch making moon-shaped cakes and baking them, saying:

I do not bake the bread nor the salt, nor do I cook the honey with the wine. I bake the Body and Blood and the Soul of Great Diana . . . O Diana! In honour of thee I will hold a feast. . . .

When the cakes are cooked they are to be partaken of at a 'Great Feast' ending in sexual high jinks:

. . . All shall sit down to Supper. And the Great Feast over, they shall dance and sing and make music and then love in the darkness with all the lights extinguished – for it is the Great Diana who extinguishes them.

Who compiled the *Book of Shadows*? Probably Gardner himself, but one of us has heard a number of reports that Aleister Crowley had a hand in it, receiving a fee from Gardner for his services. There is some internal evidence in the book that tends to support this belief. Thus a portion of the book is called 'The Charge'. This is regarded as peculiarly holy by many contemporary witches and is often recited at coven meetings. Most of it is identical with passages in a book written in the last century by C.G. Leland. One part of it, however, reads as follows:

> I am the gracious Goddess who gives the gift of joy unto the heart of Man. Upon earth I give unimaginable joys; upon death I give peace, rest and ecstasy. Nor do I demand aught in sacrifice.

The wording has a strong resemblance to Chapter 1, v. 58 of Crowley's *Book of the Law*:

> I give unimaginable joys on earth: certainty, not faith, while in life, upon death; peace unutterable, rest, ecstasy; nor do I demand aught in sacrifice.

Some of those whom Gardner initiated into witchcraft established covens of their own. Such covens, and others derived from them, still survive, and 'Gardnerian' witches are to be found in both Europe and the USA.

There are three grades of witches in these groups. They are, in ascending order of supposed magical attainment: 1) First Degree – Priest (or Priestess) and Witch; 2) Second Degree – Magus, if a man, Witch Queen if a woman; 3) Third Degree – High Priest or Priestess.

The initiation to the First Degree involves the candidate, nude, blind folded and with hands tied, being led into the 'Circle of Power', where he or she receives the 'five-fold kiss' (on feet, knees, genitals, breast, and lips) and is scourged. An oath of secrecy is then administered, following which the witch receives the 'tools of art' – magical weapons which include a black-handled knife, 'the athame', supposedly capable of 'dominating, enslaving and punishing all rebellious spirits and demons'.

The initiation to the Second Degree also involves scourging, but the high point of the ceremony is the recital, or sometimes the enactment as a short mystery play, of the 'legend of the Goddess'. This is a variant of the Greek

Half-human, half-animal creatures riding to the Witches' Sabbath. (Ulrich Molitor, *De Laniis et Phitonicis Mulieribus*, 1489.)

myth concerning Persephone in the Hades and ends with the words:

> There are three great events in the life of Man; Love, Death and Resurrection in a new body. Magic rules them all. For to make Love perfect you must return at the same time and place as the loved one, remember the past and love again.

The rite concludes with the candidate being led around the Circle and the announcement to the 'Mighty Ones of the Elements' that a new Witch Queen (or Magus) has been consecrated.

The Third Degree is centred around ritual copulation between the candidate and his or her initiator. The details of this are of little interest – from the point of view of occultism at any rate. Some covens have replaced physical with symbolic sex; a magic knife is inserted into a cup of wine and the coven is informed that 'as is the Woman to the Man so is the cup to the athamé'.

Eight main festivals are celebrated by Gardnerian witches – May Eve, All Hallows' Eve, Candlemas (2 February), Lammas (2 August), the two equinoxes and the two solstices. There are some variations in the ceremonies from one coven to another, but the following outline of the instruction for the Candlemas rite is fairly typical:

> Proceed to the site with a dance step, waving brooms and lighted torches; the High Priestess carries a broomstick shaped like an erect phallus. All, dancing, form the Magic Circle. The High Priest enters, in his right hand the consecrated magic sword, in his left hand the wooden image of an erect phallus. Priest and Priestess exchange the five-fold kiss; the Priestess then invokes the god into the Priest with the invocation, 'Dread Lord of Death and Resurrection, Lord of Life, Giver of Life, Thou Whose Name is Mystery of Mysteries, encourage our hearts. Let thy Light crystallise in our blood, bringing us to Resurrection. For there is no part of us that is not of the gods! Descend, we pray thee, upon thy servant and Priest'. Following the descent of the god

into the Priest have the Cakes and Wine ceremony, the Great Rite, a feast and a communal dance.

The 'Cakes and Wine ceremony' is a sort of witch cult sacrament. Wine and crescent-shaped cakes (compounded of wine, meal, honey, oil, salt and sometimes blood) are blessed by the High Priestess and ritually consumed by all those participating in the festival. The 'Great Rite' – believed by Gardnerian witches to be the most potent of magical techniques – is sexual intercourse between Priest and Priestess.

Gardner died in 1964 and since then modern witchcraft has suffered much fragmentation. Some covens have played down the sexual aspects of the cult, others have emphasised them, using magic and religion in a way that most outsiders would regard as merely a camouflage for sado-masochistic group sex.

Other covens, claiming that they do not derive from Gardner, have been active in the last fifteen years or so. Many of these came into existence as the result of the activities of Mr. Alex Sanders, who was an extremely active 'King of the Witches' in the late '60s and early '70s. Witches initiated by Mr. Sanders or one of his many disciples are usually referred to as Alexandrians. They use a *Book of Shadows* more or less identical with that used by Gardner's followers but many of them have also experimented with more formal ceremonial magic of the Golden Dawn variety.

The most interesting groups of contemporary witches are those known as the 'robed covens'. These eschew nudity in their workings, often display an attitude of contempt towards Alexandrian and Gardnerian witchcraft, and claim to have derived their craft from sources unknown to either Gerald Gardner or Alex Sanders. There is much diversity amongst these covens. Some of them have abandoned magical workings of any type and have become eccentric pagan groups worshipping old Norse or Celtic deities. Others – of which the composite Aradia Coven of our first chapter is typical – show signs of developing into occult fraternities.

In recent years there has been much less press coverage of modern witches and their activities than was previously the case. Possibly this indicates a decline in numbers. More probably it results from a lessening public interest in the cult following what was, in every sense of the phrase, considerable over-exposure.

15 *Pathway into The Darkness of Time*

What induces people to practise witchcraft and ceremonial magic? Why, in an age which is so devoted to 'openness', to 'freedom of information', and to other liberal panaceas, do men and women who are interested in the paranormal tend to join small secret groups rather than being totally open in their activities?

There are undoubtedly sociological and psychological factors involved. If one feels an inner inadequacy and uncertainty about oneself and one's place in the society in which one lives there is something very attractive about being part of an 'in-group', whether that group is an occult association or an extremist political *groupuscle*. Again, if an individual has difficulty in coping with the everyday business of living it is pleasant for that individual to compensate for this by feeling that he or she is possessed of mysterious powers.

But such explanations are only partially true, for the rebirth of Western magic and alchemy is not an isolated phenomenon. It is, as we have remarked earlier, a part of an 'esoteric explosion', a boom in minority religions and philosophical beliefs and practices that shows itself in many ways. In, for example, the popularity of yoga and other spiritual disciplines of oriental origin, in the spread of fringe medicine, in Flying Saucer cults, and in the growth of new religions such as Subud and Scientology. Throughout the Western world substantial numbers of people are abandoning traditional beliefs – moral, religious and cultural – and adopting others which are, it could be argued, alien, eccentric, and even dangerous.

There have been other 'occult booms' in Western history; in, for example, the renaissance. But to find anything comparable to what is happening at the present time one has to go back to the last centuries of classical paganism. Then philosophers practised theurgy, the art supposed to enable men and gods to communicate with one another, then Chaldean *mathematici* and other soothsayers flourished, then strange Asiatic religions had their devotees as far afield as Britain and France. Eventually the most vital of these latter cults, Christianity, captured the machinery of the state and began to destroy rivals. Almost simultaneously the barbarian invasions which had begun a century before increased in number and virulence.

Modern magicians (Doug Armstrong).

Eventually the state of which the Christians had gained control was swept away; with it vanished, paradoxically enough, most of the magicians and *mathematici* it had persecuted.

Perhaps the same thing will happen again. A new religion may become the dominant intellectual force in Western society, and then that same society, intellectually, morally and artistically exhausted, may be destroyed by some new barbarian invasion – perhaps by the armoured legions of the rulers of what was once Holy Russia.

But whatever the future holds it is likely that in some form or another magic will survive. For in spite of all the charlatanism and madness that has been associated with the rebirth of magic there is no doubt that it has appealed to some of humanity's deepest instincts. The nature and importance of this appeal was summed up, over a century ago, by the bibliographer Charles Nodier:

> . . . it is impossible to deny or affirm things which do not fit in with the little rules of our little minds. The occult sciences have their roots too far in the past, and they have aroused too much interest throughout the history of mankind, for them to be meaningless. . . . here is a pathway to be explored leading back into the darkness of time. Madness may be at the end, or perhaps the supreme wisdom; it is a dangerous way, but triumph would not be without its reward. . . . if a man can recapture in the mirror of memory the fugitive images of the past, he may well be able, either through some evolution in his being, or through the resurrection of a forgotten science, to create or rediscover some means to illuminate the future, the other face of the eternal Janus.

Further Reading

Those who wish to make a detailed study of the techniques which have been employed by those most active in the rebirth of magic should first read one or more general introductions to the theory and practice of magic. Several of these are easily available; perhaps the best is Richard Cavendish's *The Black Arts*, originally published by Routledge in 1967 and reprinted many times in paperback form.

Once the reader has got some grasp of the subject he would be well advised to study the writings of modern magicians. Among these we would recommend:

Crowley, Aleister, *Magick in Theory and Practice* (various editions available)
Fortune, Dion, *The Mystical Qabalah* (various editions available)
Gray, William, *Magical Ritual Methods* (Helios Books, 1969)
Regardie, Israel, *Tree of Life* (various editions available)
Art and Meaning of Magic (various editions available)
Art of True Healing (various editions available)
The Middle Pillar (various editions available)

As far as the historical background of the rebirth of magic that began with Lévi is concerned a large amount of published material is available – much of it worthless. Currently in print and well worth reading are:

Cavendish, Richard, *History of Magic* (Weidenfeld)
McIntosh, Christopher *The Rosy Cross Unveiled* (Aquarian, 1980)

There is no full biography of Lévi in English – although in French there is a hostile study by Charuel – but Christopher McIntosh's *Eliphas Lévi and the French Occult Revival* (Rider, London) is both readable and informative. Many of Lévi's own writings are available in English translation, notably *The Key of the Mysteries, Transcendental Magic* and *The History of Magic*. The latter work admirably illustrates Lévi's romanticism, although worthless as history.

While there is much printed material in French on the subject of Lévi's disciples and other French occultists there is very little available in English save for the previously mentioned book by Mr. McIntosh and the late Robert Baldick's *J.K. Huysmans* (Clarendon Press, 1954).

As will be apparent to the readers of this book it is the Golden Dawn that has been the 'fount and origin' of the rebirth of magic, and some knowledge of its rituals and teachings is essential for the occult student. Most of these are included in the four volumes of Israel Regardie's *Golden Dawn*, reprinted several times in recent years by Llewellyn Publications of Minnesota. Further original Golden Dawn material can be found in *Astral Projection, Magic and Alchemy* by S.L. MacGregor Mathers (Spearman, London, and Wiser, New York, 1971). As far as the history of the order is concerned the only book that can be unreservedly recommended is Ellic Howe's *The Magicians of the Golden Dawn* (Routledge).

There is a wealth of published material on the life and teachings of Aleister Crowley. His own *Confessions* have been published by Bantam, John Symond's *The Great Beast* is useful in spite of its unsympathetic tone, and some have found F. King's *The Magical World of Aleister Crowley* worth reading. Israel Regardie's *The Eye in the*

Triangle (Llewellyn, 1970) is probably destined to remain the definitive study of Crowley's intellectual development. Most of Crowley's magical writings are either still in print or easily available in the second-hand market.

Dion Fortune's books are mostly still in print, but so far no biography of her has been published.

Notes

Chapter One

(1) Most modern magicians interpret such 'invisibility' as being not some sort of transparency but merely obscurity.

(2) In his *The Rosy Cross Unveiled* (Aquarian, 1980)

Chapter Two

(1) The phrase 'astral' (i.e., 'starry') body was originated by Paracelsus who believed it was the medium through which the heavenly bodies transmitted their supposed influence to men and women.

Chapter Four

(1) This story, told by Philostratus, provided Keats with the inspiration for his *Lamia*.

(2) For a description of this Lullean 'machine' see James Blish's occult novel *Black Easter*.

(3) This 17th century translation of Paracelsus' *Archidoxes Magicae* has recently been reprinted by Askin Publishers under the title *Archidoxıs of Magic*.

Chapter Six

(1) 'After Bacchus, Venus; after Venus, Mercury' was a popular Victorian medical student's joke.

Chapter Seven

(1) The full text of the instruction which contains this passage can be found in Dr. Regardie's *Golden Dawn*.

Chapter Eight

(1) This letter was written to F.L. Gardner. For some description of Gardner's voluminous correspondence see E. Howe's *Magicians of the Golden Dawn*.

Chapter Nine

(1) See her 'Lightbearers of Darkness' (n.d.), a collection of articles published by her in *The Patriot*.

Chapter Eleven

(1) 'Samhain' – i.e., All Saints' Eve.

(2) In fact these were German pietists with only a tenuous Rosicrucian connection.

THE NECRONOMICON

Edited by George Hay
Introduced by Colin Wilson
Researched by Robert Turner and David Langford

Connoisseurs of the occult have for years been tantalised by references — especially in the works of H.P. Lovecraft — to a mysterious book, allegedly written by a visionary Arab philosopher, which was stated to convey the most shocking truths about mankind's true origin.

Thanks to years of research by such experts in the occult field as L. Sprague de Camp, Angela Carter, Dr. Christopher Frayling and Colin Wilson,

THAT BOOK HAS NOW BEEN FOUND . . .

THE NECRONOMICON

THE BOOK OF DEAD NAMES

the lost masterpiece of occult literature and a disturbing account of the dark side of creation.

0 552 98093 5 £1.25

LIFE AFTER LIFE
by RAYMOND A. MOODY, JR., M.D.

A man is dying and, as he reaches the point of greatest physical distress, he hears himself pronounced dead by his doctor. He begins to hear an uncomfortable noise, a loud ringing or buzzing, and at the same time feels himself moving very rapidly through a long, dark tunnel. After this, he finds himself outside of his own physical body . . . Soon, other things begin to happen. Others come to meet and help him. He glimpses the spirits of relatives and friends who have already died, and a loving, warm spirit of a kind he has never encountered before — *a being of light* — appears before him.

Over the past five years, Dr. Raymond Moody has studied more than one hundred subjects who have experienced "clinical death" and been revived. Their accounts of this experience are startingly similar in detail.

"It is research like Dr. Moody presents in his book that will enlighten many and will confirm what we have been taught for two thousand years — that there is life after death."

— From the foreword by Elisabeth Kubler-Ross, M.D.

0 553 1409 2 £1.00

ALSO AVAILABLE BY THE SAME AUTHOR:

REFLECTIONS ON LIFE AFTER LIFE

Further investigation of an extraordinary phenomenon — survival of life after bodily death.

0 553 11140 X £1.00

GHOSTS OF WALES
by PETER UNDERWOOD

Wales has many ghosts and amid the beauty of its vales and hills, its towns and villages and hamlets, there are literally hundreds of haunted spots. Peter Underwood, the eminent psychical researcher and well-known broadcaster, travels through the country, walking where shadowy phantom figures have walked, talking where ghostly voices have talked, driving where ghost coach-and-horses have driven and pausing where ghosts have paused before him. From Aberaeron in Dyfed to Welshpool in Powis, and many stops along the way, the reader is introduced to a region whose folklore and daily life is more visited by the occult than anywhere else in the British Isles.

0 552 11315 8 £1.25

THE AIRMEN WHO WOULD NOT DIE
by JOHN G. FULLER

In 1928, as the Graf Zeppelin prepared to fly around the world, the British raced to complete the luxurious R 101 airship that was to revolutionize air travel. In spite of severe structural problems, the government had decided that the take-off date could not be postponed — for British pride was at stake . . .

Nor would they heed the detailed, fearsome warning from a dead World War One ace — a warning from the life beyond . . .

The R 101 plunged to the ground on the French side of the Channel . . . and two days later, during a seance, the commander of the ill-fated airship related in ghastly detail, R 101's tragic end . . .

THE AIRMEN WHO WOULD NOT DIE — The spell-binding story of the airmen who came back from the grave!

'Industriously researched' NOW Magazine

'A fascinating book' THE SCOTSMAN

S.B.N. 0 552 11591 6 Price: £1.50

MIRACLES OF THE GODS
by ERICH VON DANIKEN

Today's most original investigator of the unexplained takes a penetrating look at miracles, visions and all the supernatural wonders that Churches throughout the centuries have recognised as 'holy'. What are visions? Are they supernatural phenomena, or the product of mass auto-suggestion? Can they be divine revelations, or extraterrestrial communications? Erich von Daniken's theories are far more fascinating than any one of these . . . In this latest book, the best-selling author of CHARIOTS OF THE GODS?, RETURN TO THE STARS, THE GOLD OF THE GODS and IN SEARCH OF ANCIENT GODS turns his ever-questing mind to Christianity — and the religions that reach back far beyond Christ . . .

0 552 10371 3 £1 50

THE GOLD OF THE GODS
by ERICH VON DANIKEN

On a journey covering 76,000 miles, von Daniken traced the clues to the birth of mankind and to the history of the planet Earth.

He found incredible treasures of ages past, undeciphered writings and drawings in solid gold — relics of civilisations long-dead. But he also found startling evidence to suggest that way back, before the dawn of recorded history, the Earth was host to extraterrestrial visitors who colonised our planet . . .

"Fantastic? Certainly. But very, very convincing . . ."
— SUNDAY MIRROR

0 552 09689 X £1.25

THE ANCIENT MAGIC OF THE PYRAMIDS
by KEN JOHNSON

A mystery from the ancient world tht continues to baffle the most sophisticated minds of the twentieth century . . .

Ten miles from the bustling streets of modern-day Cairo stands the sole survivors of the ancient world's Seven Wonders — the Pyramids of Giza.

For centuries, archaeologists have pondered the purpose of these awesome monuments. Were they tombs of the pharaohs? Shelters from some prehistoric cataclysm? The Biblical granaries of Joseph? Or are they repositories of the wisdom of a super-civilisation . . . a civilisation forgotten over the millennia, which created in the pyramids sophisticated generators to harness the most powerful of all energy sources — the earth itself?

A startling book that poses a riddle more tantalising than that of the sphinx!

0 552 10928 2 80p

A SELECTED LIST OF PSYCHIC, MYSTIC AND OCCULT TITLES FROM CORGI

While every effort is made to keep prices low, it is sometimes necessary to increase prices at short notice. Corgi Books reserve the right to show new retail prices on covers which may differ from those previously advertised in the text or elsewhere.

The prices shown below were correct at the time of going to press.

	No.	Title	Author	Price
☐	11567 3	THE PROPHECIES OF NOSTRADAMUS	*Erika Cheetham*	£1.75
☐	11716 1	SIGNS OF THE GODS	*Erich Von Daniken*	£1.50
☐	08800 5	CHARIOTS OF THE GODS?	*Erich Von Daniken*	£1.35
☐	09083 2	RETURN TO THE STARS	*Erich Von Daniken*	95p
☐	09689 X	THE GOLD OF THE GODS	*Erich Von Daniken*	£1.35
☐	10073 0	IN SEARCH OF ANCIENT GODS	*Erich Von Daniken*	85p
☐	10371 3	MIRACLES OF THE GODS	*Erich Von Daniken*	£1.50
☐	10870 7	ACCORDING TO THE EVIDENCE	*Erich Von Daniken*	£1.25
☐	11591 6	THE AIRMEN WHO WOULD NOT DIE	*John G. Fuller*	£1.50
☐	11020 5	THE GHOST OF FLIGHT 401	*John G. Fuller*	£1.50
☐	09430 7	THE U.F.O. EXPERIENCE — A SCIENTIFIC INQUIRY	*J. Allen Hynek*	95p
☐	10928 2	THE ANCIENT MAGIC OF THE PYRAMIDS	*Ken Johnson*	80p
☐	14609 2	LIFE AFTER LIFE	*Raymond A. Moody Jr. M.D.*	£10
☐	11140 X	REFLECTIONS ON LIFE AFTER LIFE	*Raymond A. Moody Jr. M.D.*	£1.00
☐	10707 7	THREE LIVES	*T. Lobsang Rampa*	75p
☐	10628 3	DOCTOR FROM LHASA	*T. Lobsang Rampa*	£1.25
☐	11464 2	THE CAVE OF THE ANCIENTS	*T. Lobsang Rampa*	£1.50
☐	10416 7	I BELIEVE	*T. Lobsang Rampa*	£1.25
☐	10189 3	THE SAFFRON ROBE	*T. Lobsang Rampa*	£1.25
☐	10087 0	AS IT WAS!	*T. Lobsang Rampa*	£1.00
☐	09834 5	THE THIRD EYE	*T. Lobsang Rampa*	£1.25
☐	11413 8	THE RAMPA STORY	*T. Lobsang Rampa*	95p
☐	11283 6	AUTUMN LADY	*Mama San Ra-Ab Rampa*	85p

ORDER FORM

All these books are available at your book shop or newsagent, or can be ordered direct from the publisher. Just tick the titles you want and fill in the form below.

CORGI BOOKS, Cash Sales Department, P.O. Box 11, Falmouth, Cornwall.

Please send cheque or postal order, no currency.

Please allow cost of book(s) plus the following for postage and packing:

U.K. Customers—Allow 40p for the first book, 18p for the second book and 13p for each additional book ordered, to a maximum charge of £1.49.

B.F.P.O. and Eire—Allow 40p for the first book, 18p for the second book plus 13p per copy for the next 3 books, thereafter 7p per book.

Overseas Customers—Allow 60p for the first book and 18p per copy for each additional book.

NAME (block letters) ....

ADDRESS ....

....